connect

how to use data and experience marketing to create lifetime customers

lars birkholm petersen

ron person

christopher nash

WILEY

Published by John Wiley & Sons, Inc., Hoboken, New Jersey.
Published simultaneously in Canada.

For general information about our other products and services, please contact our Customer Care Department within the United States at (800) 762-2974, outside the United States at (317) 572-3993 or fax (317) 572-4002.

Wiley publishes in a variety of print and electronic formats and by print-on-demand. Some material included with standard print versions of this book may not be included in e-books or in print-on-demand. If this book refers to media such as a CD or DVD that is not included in the version you purchased, you may download this material at http://booksupport.wiley.com. For more information about Wiley products, visit www.wiley.com.

Library of Congress Cataloging-in-Publication Data:

Petersen, Lars Birkholm.
  Connect: how to use data and experience marketing to create lifetime customers / Lars Birkholm Petersen, Ron Person, Christopher Nash.
    pages cm
  Includes bibliographical references and index.
  ISBN 978-1-118-96361-6 (hardback); ISBN 978-1-118-96360-9 (ebk); ISBN 978-1-118-96362-3 (ebk)
  1. Internet marketing. 2. Customer relations. I. Person, Ron, 1948- II. Nash, Christopher. III. Title.
  HF5415.1265.P486 2014
  658.8'72—dc23

                                                                    2014025611

Printed in the United States of America

10 9 8 7 6 5 4 3

CONTENTS

The authors will donate all royalties from this book to selected charities. To learn more and help decide which charities the royalties should be donated to, visit www.ConnectTheExperience.com/charity.

FOREWORD

You cannot create experience. You must undergo it.

—Albert Camus

Many strategists realize that the world is only becoming more connected, not less. Yet many executives still wonder when all of these crazy texting, selfie-taking, snapchatting, lunch-tweeting shenanigans are going to finally fizzle out. I don't know about you, but I'm already dusting off my rotary phone and digging out my floppy disk collection just in case we do decide to go backward.

Not really.

You get it. I get it. Do we really need yet another pep rally to celebrate our like-minded perspectives and passion to bring about change? Yes. In fact, we need to ready ourselves to march the significance of the changing customer right on up to the C-suite to drive home the importance of customer-centricity not only for the benefit of people but also for the future of our business as well as our place in the market.

See, customers in all of their connected glory are evolving with or without us. At the same time there's a mind-boggling lack of urgency and a resulting sparsity of support, resources, and budget to understand and engage this rising connected customer.

Ladies and gentlemen, we have ourselves a customer experience (CX) imperative. But before we go any further, I must press pause for a moment to share something stark yet common-sensical: technology alone isn't the answer. That's right. Even though we're faced with radical changes in customer behaviors, expectations, and preferences as a result of technology, to lead the next generation of customer experience does not begin with technology. It starts with people.

Therefore, the opportunity for customer experience requires elevated discussions where organizations assess current experiences against a vision for what they can and should be. For example, is today's customer experience a by-product of our brand promise? Do we deliver against our stated intentions, and is that experience reinforced at every touch point?

Approaching customer experience in this fashion takes what is typically today a bottom-up approach and shifts decision making to a top-down model. And we all know that true transformation comes from the top. The difference, though, is that implementing customer experience initiatives with both top-down and bottom-up strategies sets the foundation on which customer-centricity can build and flourish. One is directional, the North Star if you will, where customer experience initiatives map against a vision for how brand promises are enlivened and reinforced before, during, and after transactions. It sets the standard for investments in technology, engagement, insights, and pilots. It also sets the standard to follow and the benchmark to measure against for all those who are responsible for the experience, wherever and whenever it's formed or affected.

The result is a brand promise that's measured by the experience that customers have and share. It ladders up the importance of customer experience, transcending it from a functional role to that of an enterprise-wide philosophy.

Good intentions are just the beginning, but they are not enough.

Let's assume that businesses, for the most part, want to do the right thing. After all, they're making increasing investments in customer relationship management (CRM), social, mobile, digital, etc. With spending comes sincerity and intention, right? After all my years of advising executives and researching the evolution of markets, I can honestly say that executives seem to care. I can't say that I've ever heard anything from executives indicating any intention of dethroning the customer as king.

I can't imagine sitting in a boardroom and hearing leadership reveal a new direction of anti-customer-centricity: "Team, we just don't care about our customers. And to be honest, we couldn't care less about their experience. We believe this to be a shorter, sweeter path to profitability and earn-outs."

Depending on which definition you align with, customer experience is often characterized by the perception a customer has after engaging with a company, brand, product, or service.[1]

If customer experience is a critical pillar to build relationships and business outcomes, why is it that we are still fighting the good fight? If so many executives agree that the future of business lies in customer experience, why are we spending this time together right now? What's the point? The answer is that there's a disconnect. The link between aspiration and intention is separated by vision and action.

To my surprise (well, not really), a recent study[2] found that only 37 percent of executives are actually beginning to move forward with a formal customer experience initiative. Considering that businesses race along with the speed and agility of a cinder block, I'm sure that even this initial group of leading businesses will not make significant progress to establish a competitive edge any day soon. But some companies will aggressively invest in CX and innovation in products, processes, and services, and that will set the stage for disruption.

Why?

The customer landscape is shifting. It always does. This time, however, the door to digital Darwinism has been kicked off its hinges. Technology and society are evolving faster than the ability to adapt. Consumers are becoming more connected. As such, they're more informed. With information comes empowerment. And with newfound connectedness and power, customer expectations begin to shatter current sales, marketing, and support models.

Social, mobile, and real-time connectivity each contribute to a new reality for customer experiences and engagement. This isn't news. In the previously referenced study, researchers found that 81 percent of executives agree that social media is critical for success, yet 35 percent don't support social media for sales or service.

Businesses either adapt or die. Ignoring this fact hastens digital Darwinism. Jumping in without understanding or intention is a moon shot without aiming for the moon.

This isn't just a channel strategy.

This isn't just a technology play.

This is a shift toward a new movement where customer experience now screams for us to "Create experiences!"

Indeed, customer experience happens with or without you.

The customer experience imperative needs you to make the business case.

In your organization, people are talking about customer experience right now. But for some reason it's just not a priority. Actions don't reflect promises. In CX, you must create a sense of urgency to accelerate to match or outpace the speed of market transformation. Without doing so, a sense of urgency will be created from the outside in.

It's not just about the customers you have today; those who are not already your customers represent your future growth.

Connect will help you get ahead in the new marketing revolution. Even though your customers are in control, you don't have to react to them. Lead them. In doing so, you'll learn to transform your customers' experiences, create lifetime connections with your customers, and jump ahead of your competitors.

When you take a new approach to engagement, customers feel the difference, and you feel the difference.

Nothing begins without you ... and that is why you are the hero and this is your journey. The future of digital marketing and customer experience is in your hands. Feel it. Design it. Advance it.

If you don't lead it, who will?

Brian Solis
Digital analyst and anthropologist, and
author of the best sellers, *What's the Future of Business?* (*WTF*)
and *The End of Business as Usual*

NOTES

1. http://searchcio.techtarget.com/definition/consumer-experience-CX.
2. www.oracle.com/us/corporate/features/cx-survey/index.html?goback= .gde_4702653_member_211619147#!.

INTRODUCTION

Marketing in all organizations is at a crossroads. There is a *big* revolution happening right now in consumer and business buying behavior. Gone are the days when your marketing is seen as a trusted source. No longer can you dictate customer behavior or the customer buying process. Face it—customers are in control. As a marketer, you need to understand and adapt to these rapidly changing behaviors, if there is any hope to regain credibility and become meaningful again to today's connected customer. Let me tell you how this revolution impacted me personally and how my cell phone provider lost a lifetime customer.

My second daughter was born at 12:07 A.M. Luckily the birth went well, but, being in love with technology, I was also watching the clock as the new iPhone was released at 12:01 A.M. My daughter quickly fell asleep and I found a moment to use my smartphone to browse the web store of one of the biggest cell phone carriers. I spent the next 25 minutes ordering the new iPhone. It should have been an easy task, using a smartphone to shop for a smartphone. But the experience wasn't optimized for my smartphone, even though it was a smartphone that I was shopping for. In an age when Cyber Monday nets 17 percent of all online purchases on mobile devices,[1] this was inexcusable. But I was determined—I needed the newest member of the iPhone family, and I was willing to go through the extra-painful experience of zooming and shrinking to get the task done.

Finally, I got my iPhone, and about a month later I received a newsletter from the carrier, promoting "Lars, buy the new iPhone." Surprised at how irrelevant this was to me because I had already bought the iPhone through the same vendor, I replied and asked if this was a mistake.

There was no mistake about the attitude I got back in the reply: "No, this is not a mistake; this is a mail we send to all our customers."

Here's the problem with getting a reply like this and why this newsletter upset me in the first place: the vendor is demonstrating that they doesn't know me and certainly doesn't value me as a customer. This isn't how we want to be treated as people. The last thing I want is to be treated like just another number in a customer database being marketed to by the vendor. I don't want to be marketed to if it's not something I feel is relevant to my needs.

Organizations that are doing this have not only failed to adapt, but they are in danger of losing the last shred of credibility through their marketing. Rather than connecting with customers, they are disconnecting from their customers at a blistering pace.

As a professional, I'm a busy guy, so as a consumer I need and expect the brands I deal with to be able to offer me increasingly relevant information and offers. What I want is the same experience I get when I visit the local department store, where the clerk remembers me, asks about my experiences with my last purchase, and comes back with relevant recommendations based on our dialogue. That makes me feel a connection to the store, almost to the point where I feel guilty if I don't go there to make my purchases. It's that type of relevance that keeps me coming back, because it makes me feel that the store and its personnel value my business by looking out for me and wanting to help me. It makes me as a customer feel connected with them and I happily advise my friends to buy at the same store.

I had no problem switching to a new cell phone carrier, just as I have no problem changing brands for TVs, supermarkets, and the like. There's just no loyalty there. These things are commodities in my mind. But I would not change my insurance provider, who made it personal and connected, and whose people have managed to transcend the customer relationship beyond a commodity transaction by recognizing me when I call. They give me relevant information and they even send me birthday cards with savings on products they know I want and need. Yes, I know most of it is automated and done by using data, but it shows me they know who I am and our relationship has substance.

Stories like this are daily occurrences for all of us. Consumers are taking charge and expect more meaningful experiences from organizations and marketing. Customers expect their experiences to parallel the way they interact with other people, where they aren't assaulted by mindless robotic marketing, but rather engaged in a human way that is centered on everything that makes a customer feel connected to your brand. Experience marketing is helping organizations to better understand their customers and interact with them in that human, friendly way.

Organizations today are at one of the most significant crossroads ever: taking the "business as usual" road will mean the same old generic "one size fits all" content as usual at each customer touch point, delivering largely indifferent customer experiences. The other road, the road to rich customer relevance and humanized marketing, will not be an easy road—there will be many changes needed with new processes and new relationships between organizational units. It's not easy, but the payoff is huge: you win the hearts and minds of customers and build long-term relationships that endure having impact on retaining and creating vocal customers. So it could be hard work, but it will put your organization on the path to connecting with your customers and building relationships for life. Marketing is an important stakeholder in this process, but only one part—other parts that will contribute to the connected experience are sales, service, finance, and so on, all with a big impact on the total experience. In many cases this will start as a marketing revolution that over the longer term will transform marketing into being involved in measuring and improving every business function that touches customers.

This book helps you take the right road to lifetime customers. It gives you a staged approach on how to steer your organization on this path. Whether you are in business-to-business (B2B), business-to-consumer (B2C), retail, nonprofit, government, or e-commerce work, this book is relevant for you.

Whether you are an executive or involved in day-to-day operations, this book serves as a guide, with recommendations, initiatives, work-arounds, and step-by-step processes on how you can move your team to a higher level of marketing excellence. The authors of this book have extensive experience, through our daily work in Sitecore's Business Optimization Services team, advising and consulting with many midsize, large, and global corporations. What we share in this book are the best practices we've learned through sheer hard work at countless customers around the world. This is the secret sauce in the recipe for marketing success in this rapidly evolving era of the connected customer.

WHAT YOU WILL LEARN IN THIS BOOK

Using tactics shared in this book, you will learn how:

- A retirement savings fund increased its member acquisitions.

- An airline increased online sales conversions.

- A car manufacturer increased requests for test drives.

- A pharmaceutical company uses personalization to disrupt traditional patient care and support.

Along with this book you have access to a website, www.Connect TheExperience.com, where you will find updated content, access to our frameworks, high-resolution illustrations, templates, organizational assessments, and calculators that will help you become more connected and relevant to your customers.

We hope you enjoy reading this book, but most important, we hope you find valuable best practices you can use in your marketing to serve your customers and organization better.

Lars Birkholm Petersen

TERMS AND PHRASES WE USE IN THIS BOOK

This book shows how you can take advantage of a marketing revolution affecting all types of businesses and organizations. With so many forms of business and organizational types, we have had to use terms that differ among industries, for-profit and nonprofit, and B2B and B2C. The following short reference can help you understand the terms we use.

Digital marketing is marketing. Our focus is mainly digital, as digital is the enabler of building rich customer experiences. Digital marketing is typically the starting point for organizations during this transformation, connecting key digital channels used by customers, like web, email, mobile, and social. As your organization matures, connecting to your customers and creating a great customer experience will expand to cover more channels, like points of sale, call centers, and sales, and you will be able to share more data across different organizational units.

Customer. In this book we use the term *customer*, but the term can refer to a prospective customer, a visitor on the website, or a citizen looking for the right form on a state website.

Customer experience and connected customer experience. When we refer to customer experience or connected customer experience, the term means being relevant for the customers throughout their journey, whether it's a retail customer's decision journey or a long-term high-value customer across multiple touch points.

Organization or brand. When we refer to organization or brand, this also could be your municipality, your organization, or your branded product line.

Decision journey. Throughout the book we refer to the decision journey, which is the decision and commitment process the customer uses to make a commitment or purchase. In many organizations—for example, hospitals, municipalities, activist nonprofits—you aren't selling products, but a decision and commitment are still necessary. By decision and commitment we are simply referring to the point where the customer moves to the next step of engagement with the product and/or service. For example, this could be as simple as getting a customer to fill out an online form.

For most organizations, branding and loyalty are critical. In those cases the decision journey continues through to creating a lifetime of commitment.

REQUEST FOR FEEDBACK

We love helping organizations adapt to the needs of the connected customer by building meaningful and connected customer experiences. We would like to get your feedback on our thoughts and practices in this book, as well as to learn what is working well, what isn't working, or missing pieces that should have been in this book.

We can be contacted at authors@ConnectTheExperience.com or by using #ConnectCX for any feedback or questions you might have.

NOTE

1. "Cyber Monday Report 2013," IBM, December 2013.

CHAPTER 1

The Customer Is in Control

The only thing that is constant is change.

—Heraclitus

The stakes have never been higher for marketing; to win the marketing game is to transform marketing into one of the most important drivers in achieving business objectives. To lose or even fall behind in marketing could result in your organization dropping back as your competitors take control.

Organizations and marketers need to adapt to, take advantage of, and stay at the leading edge of emerging technology. Marketers need to use technology as a competitive advantage, like Netflix eating Blockbuster's market share or Amazon.com changing first how we buy books, then changing how we buy retail products, and now disrupting everyday shopping with the Amazon Dash. Marketers who aren't ready to adapt and use the new technology will be left behind.

As a marketer, these are very exciting times—we are in the midst of a marketing revolution and we get to influence the outcome. Making the right decisions now and acting on them will not only help achieve your business objectives, but will also increase your marketing skills, your personal expertise, and your professional value.

Traditional marketing is fading away and will soon disappear altogether. This is the legacy marketing strategy where the approach was to broadcast a generic set of marketing messages to large groups of customers in different channels, like television, billboards, web, email, and social. Even when the messages across different channels were related, the experience of the customer across different channels was not.

You experience this type of disjointed marketing every day. For example:

- You see an ad banner on a mobile website and click it to find out the experience isn't optimized for mobile and has little to do with the original offer.

- You buy a product online and later get an email or see display ads promoting the product you just bought.

- You watch and "like" a video on a website and later get an email to watch that video again.

This isn't to say that traditional marketing doesn't serve a purpose. It continues to build awareness and it can educate. Traditional marketing was very effective in its heyday. Just think of the old 1950s commercials—they aimed at educating consumers to buy products from big brands. But that marketing isn't broadly effective anymore. Here's why.

WELCOME TO THE ERA OF THE CONNECTED CUSTOMER

What we have seen in the past 10 years is a revolution in how customers are able to connect with peers and share information—information about your brand like discussions, recommendations, and reviews.

This information has always been out there, but with the rise of Internet publishing and social networks, more information is easily accessible, and individual consumers have an unprecedented ability to broadcast their experiences with little to no effort. Where it took a lot of time and effort 10 years ago to research about products, services, and how other people experience them, it now takes next to none.

Fundamentally, customers haven't changed, but how they decide has changed. In fact, CEB (Corporate Executive Board Company) found that business-to-business (B2B) buyers are 57 percent through the purchase decision before engaging with sales.[1] That's why it's more important than ever to have connected marketing that is relevant to customers' needs across the myriad of channels they use for research. Your brand must be in the customer's top of mind (preferably unassisted) so that it is at the beginning of the decision journey and one of the products the customer searches for before reaching out to sales.

THE FUTURE

The bad news for marketing is that the rate of change isn't slowing down. The marketers who adapt as rapidly as consumers will disrupt industry segments and steal market share from their competitors. Just look at how Airbnb is changing how customers find travel accommodations, what Uber has done to taxis and car services in cities, or what Esurance has done to the insurance industry. As a marketer, you will always be playing catch-up to the next agile marketer; and if that is taken with a losing attitude, it is a terrible position to be in. But take it with a winning attitude and it's great—it gives the agile marketer a chance to continually innovate and move ahead.

If marketing is to be effective, we must create a culture of connected marketing. Connected marketing demands that marketing align with customers by using their preferred channel for communication, heeding what your customers are telling you in their interactions with you, and demonstrating that knowledge by engaging them with relevant content and appropriate offers in their preferred channel for communication. Marketing must be faster and more agile than in the past, ready to move rapidly to emerging channels of communication, and constantly staying in tune with our customers.

This is experience marketing. This next generation of marketing provides marketers with a single view of the customer in real-time so that marketers can personalize every experience, across all channels.

TRUST AS THE NEW CURRENCY

How can we align how we sell with how customers decide?

First we need to acknowledge that the traditional marketing funnel is fading as marketing's first approach; with the increased use of different channels, marketing needs to be pervasive throughout the customer journey.

To better understand how customers decide, we need to understand the different groups of customers and their different intents, motivations, emotions, and decision journeys throughout the different stages of the customer journey. Depending on their objectives, some customers might be very methodical in their research, while others could be more spontaneous. Some will rely on social proof and liking, whereas others will try to be the trendsetters, others will be early adopters, and still others will use the brand as a statement for who they are.

The better we understand the different people we are marketing to, the better we can align messages and build relationships.

Customers go through different stages in their journey. In most cases their journey looks like Figure 1.1.

Figure 1.1   Stages of Customer Journey

As customers take more control of their journey their decision point moves closer to the purchase stage. That pushes customers need to contact sales farther down the journey. Most customers will reach out to sales late in the research stage or early in the decide stage. If marketers wait until these late stages to engage with customers, there is little time to influence the buying decision.

One of marketing's key roles is to move that point of contact earlier in the customer journey. To do that we need to build trust with the customer by aligning content with the customer's stage in the decision journey. Pushing the wrong content, offers, or communication at the wrong stage can destroy the marketing-customer relationship. At the earliest stages it's not about product features but more about the value and benefits of that product, with which the customer can identify.

It's also important to understand that a customer's willingness to engage changes over the decision journey. As a first-time visitor on a car website, most customers won't give access to personal details right away, unless it's relevant. At the different points of interaction, customers exchange different amounts and levels of information. The more specific information the customer needs, the more personal information the customer is willing to exchange. As a first-time visitor, customers are most likely browsing the market and gathering information to research and compare brands, to see which match their own values and needs. At this point the car website hasn't built enough trust with the customer, so the amount of information exchanged is limited. The customer might be willing to provide basic information such as an email address, as this is low-risk content. As the marketing information becomes more relevant, there is more credibility and trust and the customer is more willing to reveal additional information.

Different steps are necessary to achieve this information exchange. The steps for these tactics are shown in Figure 1.2.

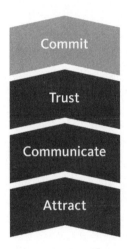

Figure 1.2   Steps to Build Trust and Commitment

Attract

You need to be able to attract customers using key messaging or calls to action in the channels preferred by customers. At this point it may be through offline channels. It might be something as huge as a billboard in a strategic location, but ideally to capture the target audience the marketing message must be relevant. This could be done via targeted ads segmented by demographics and psychographics or by intent expressed through search keywords on a search engine. This information is tied to specific individuals and is incredibly valuable and should not be lost when marketing moves from external to owned marketing channels.

Communicate

Based on the intent expressed by the customers, we marketers need to be relevant in our communication. For digital channels that means contextualizing the experience to the customer's needs, personal profile, psychological triggers, stage in the decision journey, and digital device. The more relevant our message is, both in content and context, the better conversation will be with customers and the more engaged they will be through our digital channels. Communication at the early stages of the decision journey is focused more on the customer values than on the product we are selling; we need to connect emotionally so that customers can identify themselves with our brand and want to learn more.

Trust

Relevant communication leads to establishing trust: trust of our brand and the relevant value we are able to provide. Trust will help customers revisit your channels and be increasingly more vocal about the content they have found. It's crucial to establish trust, as trust leads to commitment.

Commit

Throughout a decision journey, there can be many points of commitment, as shown in Figure 1.3. In the early stages, commitment moves the customer closer to your objectives. This could be as simple as exchanging an email address for low-risk content. Deeper into the decision journey the need for trust increases, the commitment required is greater, and you can collect more data from the customer.

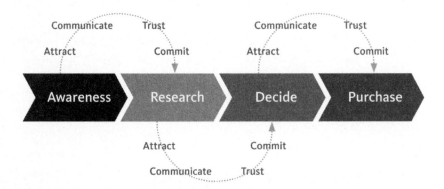

Figure 1.3   Each Touch Point Is a Chance to Build Toward Commitment

Think of the commitments as being micro and macro conversions that move the customer toward your key objectives. At each of these micro or macro points, your communication needs to be relevant and must establish trust appropriate to that point.

HOW RELEVANT ARE YOU TO YOUR CUSTOMERS?

Walk in the shoes of your customers and take our "Communicate with Intent" test.

List one of your key products or services: _____

_____

Which keyword sentence would reveal if a visitor is interested in this? (Try to avoid branded keywords.)	_____
Go to your favorite search engine and type in the sentence; list which links are found.	_____
Click on one of the links. Which content do you see? Is this relevant according to the intent expressed in the search?	[ ] Yes [ ] No
Click to the front page of the site. Is this relevant to the customer's intent?	[ ] Yes [ ] No
What are you proposing as the next step for the customer?	_____
Is this step relevant for the customer?	[ ] Yes [ ] No
Have you established enough trust for taking this step?	[ ] Yes [ ] No
Which of these do you pass?	
Attract	[ ] Yes [ ] No
Communicate	[ ] Yes [ ] No
Trust	[ ] Yes [ ] No
Commitment	[ ] Yes [ ] No

You can take the Communicate with Intent test online at this book's companion website, www.ConnectTheExperience.com/CWIT.

DATA IS THE GLUE

At every point of interaction, you exchange data with your customer. In the beginning, data from the customer is implicit and anonymous, but as the commitment increases so does the specificity of the data, and you get more access to explicit data, such as demographics and psychographics.

Accurate data is important to move the conversation to the next touch point where additional data can be captured and to be able to measure the connected experience.

For many marketing teams, this need for data at each touch point means a new approach and more data-driven marketing.

THE NEW MARKETING MANDATE: CONNECTED MARKETING IN THE ERA OF THE CONNECTED CUSTOMER

Welcome to the New Marketing Mandate, one of the most exciting times to be a marketer. You get to create a mandate that makes marketing essential to driving business outcomes. You have the chance to move marketing away from being the "poster" department to creating and executing a strategy that drives real business outcome. Through data-driven insights, you have the chance to forecast and optimize tangible business outcomes and achieve strategic business objectives.

Taking these steps will require many marketers to shift focus, assume different roles, and take new approaches. That is why we've written this book. We start with what you can do today by focusing on quick wins while helping to set the long-term vision and planning for marketing. All of this focuses on creating world-class relevant and connected customer experiences. This is a marketing approach that does more than increase your customer count; it builds customers who are your lifetime advocates.

NOTE

1. "The Digital Evolution in B2B Marketing," CEB Marketing Leadership Council, 2012.

CHAPTER 2

The New Marketing Mandate

To go far you must begin near, and the nearest step is the most important one.

—Jiddu Krishnamurti

Welcome to the age of mass personalized service.

The new frontier in marketing is not just for the Amazon.coms of the world; it's for all marketers. With today's technology, all marketers can connect with their customers. Investing in technology that helps you focus on optimizing the customer experience should be top of mind. It's affordable and it has a proven effect on improving business results. To get started most effectively, you need to focus on certain initiatives.

KEY INITIATIVES

With the New Marketing Mandate comes change. There are specific initiatives that must happen to transform your organization from a traditional marketing organization to a leading-edge one where the marketing organization is a key business driver and has an important stake in strategic decisions.

Metrics

Yesterday's technology made it difficult for marketers to access the numbers they needed to optimize their marketing. Marketers for too long relied on metrics like website visits, time on site, and page views for reporting success. Advertising was limited to metrics like impressions, frequency, and click-through rates when reporting and trying to justify its spend. There simply was no other way to get metrics and numbers that were more relevant to business objectives.

The biggest challenge with these metrics is that they don't have a direct relationship to business objectives. Because of that, they don't engage executive decision makers. Marketers have heard a patronizing, "That's nice, Joe—50,000 more visits this month; keep up the good work," when they should have instead heard, "A $1,094,342 increase in revenue this month. That's great! How can we optimize that further? What do you need to do to hit the next target, Joe?"

A key initiative that needs to happen is changing the metrics of yesterday to what really matters. We need to have a timely, relevant metric that closely correlates to our strategic objectives so the impact on business is easy to understand and recommendations are easy to make. When we work with organizations, we help them establish this metric by first identifying the most important strategic and marketing objectives. Then we identify the digital goals that drive those objectives, and create the metric that correlates with success. In Chapter 7, we dive into the metric of the future, Engagement Value, and walk through what this can do for your organization.

Customer Life Cycle Engagement

The key to building customer advocates is understanding them, their intent, what motivates them, and stages in their Customer Life Cycle (CLC). To effectively do this, you need to establish an understanding of your customer's life cycle across all your organization's business units and stakeholders. Too much focus has been only on getting to the end of the sales funnel. There should be focus on all the stages and beyond. Buying the product or service is when the real experience starts for the customer. If you don't focus on educating customers to get the most value from your brand, how can you expect them to return for repeat business and become vocal advocates?

Typical phases in the Customer Life Cycle are:

- Decision journey
- Educate

- Use

- Share

Each phase has different stages and objectives. These should be customized so they map as closely as possible to the actual stages your customers travel. What follows is a generic description of each phase of the Customer Life Cycle.

Decision Journey

The key objective in the decision journey is to get the customer to purchase your products or services. As part of the decision journey, the customers typically go through stages like need, awareness, research, compare, decide, and purchase. Along these stages, you would have micro objectives, like getting their email details or having the customers consume certain content or getting them to provide needed details, which will help the customers move forward in the decision journey. When considering these stages, it's also worth looking at the different touch points, so you can plan how you can connect different channels during the decision journey. As customers move forward in the decision journey, their intent and motivation to share data change, and the better your marketing can adapt to those changes, the more relevant the customer's experience will be.

Educate

The key objective of the educate phase is building knowledge, so customers are more aware of how to better use your products and services. For example, if they have booked a vacation, the education phase could be preparing them with tour tips or teaching them how to get the best experience at the airport or in the plane. Another example might be if they have just bought new premium headphones; then the education phase gives them the best advice for becoming familiar with the product. It's true even for services. For example, if someone is going to a doctor appointment, the doctor's staff should want to make sure the patient understands the entire process, where to park, what papers need to be signed, what will happen, what the follow-up will be, and so forth. For every type of customer and product/service relationship, there is an education phase.

The educate phase can be divided into smaller stages, like on-boarding, advice, and training. Each of these small stages will have objectives related to making sure that the customers engage and share knowledge internally with their stakeholders.

Use

The key objective of the use phase is to help your customers get the most value out of your products or services. Unlike the educate phase, which focuses on the first period after the purchase, the use phase helps the customer discover how to best use the product or services after initially onboarding.

The use phase is where customers experience your brand, via your product and services. Great experiences come from a mix of excellent support and perceived value through using the product or service. Typical increments in the use phase are discover, support, experience, and value. The primary objective is to obtain increased value from the experience with your product or service.

Share

The key objective of the share phase is getting your customers to be vocal both in terms of feeding insights back to your organization as well as advocating about your brand (giving you increased reach).

If customers perceive your product or service as valuable and a great experience, then they are more likely to share the experience with their peers. In the share stage it's important that you both encourage and facilitate what is needed to collect the feedback and allow customers to be vocal. Stages within the share phase are typically feedback, share, and advocate.

Customer Lifetime Value

Moving customers all the way through the life cycle will not only increase their Customer Lifetime Value (CLV), but it will also increase the CLVs of new customers, as the increase in brand advocates lowers the acquisition costs for new customers.

Once you map the Customer Life Cycle (CLC), your next task is to look at your different customer segments and for each segment map their journey throughout the CLC. You must understand their different needs and motives.

In Chapter 6 we give examples on how to work with Customer Life Cycles and map different customer segments to the CLC. The tool we use to map the CLC and customer groups is called the Digital Relevancy Map.

Contextualization

The third initiative is owning the experience. Customer experience is key to engaging customers and moving them forward in the decision journey and their life cycles. Customers are going to have experiences with or without your help. The question is whether those experiences will be intentional or unintentional. As a marketer, if you want intentional customer experiences, you need to own the experience. To do that, you need contextualization—the ability to change the customer's experience to meet the customer's context of need, stage, access device, and more. As the customer moves across different channels, it's important that the experience remains connected and you continue a relevant conversation across all channels.

The more you are able to adapt to the changing customer context and provide a more relevant experience across all channels, the closer connection the customer will have to your brand and offers.

Working with contextualization requires a staged approach. First it's a matter of connecting the channels that the customer uses the most and using simple tactics to maintain the context across these channels. Later it's making sure that marketing has a single view of the customer, a view that crosses all offline and online channels in real time. In Chapter 8, Optimize, we cover how to get started with contextualization.

Organizational Buy-In

The last key to success requires getting key executives on board and having them as motivated sponsors. Creating a connected experience requires buy-in and change from many organizational units because customers have many touch points with your organization. To execute and sustain that cross-organizational change requires motivation, planning, new processes, and new attitudes in business units outside of marketing. That requires buy-in at key executive positions.

Chapter 5 describes approaches to making change happen in marketing and across the entire organization. In Chapter 12, we cover different roles needed for this change, and in Chapter 13 we focus on how you can sell this to the executives and board.

DON'T BOIL THE OCEAN

Adapting the New Marketing Mandate and the initiatives needed to make it happen introduce disciplines and processes that may be new to your organization.

Although the opportunities are many with these new disciplines and processes, there are also risks. Too often we have seen projects that became too complex even before being launched. This is especially true when planning for connected experiences. With contextualization there is a risk of over complicating the discussion resulting in paralysis by analysis.

It's important to start with quick wins that are informed by data. Start with contextualization opportunities where there is a big potential, typically looking at a high volume of visitors that were lost opportunities. These can produce high gains at low marginal effort, giving you a quick win and valuable know-how for deeper contextualization. Quick wins are also a great way to gain momentum and boost motivation for your new disciplines and processes.

AGILE APPROACH FOR MARKETING

With inspiration from agile development, marketing organizations should consider how they can adopt similar benefits of using an agile approach. In short, agile development methodology has allowed teams of developers to break their large complex projects into smaller, more manageable chunks, and allows them to be more responsive to changing needs. Similarly an agile approach to marketing would allow teams to respond to constantly shifting market conditions, by making smaller and more rapid iterations instead implementing large, complex programs that take a long time to execute and have a high risk of failure. When building connected and relevant experiences with your customers, it's important to foster an agile culture that will accelerate your speed to market. Marketing should have the mandate to launch new initiatives as trends occur and to test different experiences to see what is most effective. This also means that marketing will launch experiences that will underperform, but that is fine as long as marketing remains agile and can stop those initiatives, use the knowledge, and launch new and better experiences.

Transforming marketing into an agile organization will be incremental and needs to be heavily backed by data-driven decisions.

INVESTING WHERE IT'S NEEDED

Investments are needed to get these new initiatives launched (typically there won't be a budget), as these are new disciplines. You should start with investments in digital marketing, as this is the enabler of connected experiences, but remember that customer experiences are across your entire organization. As your entire organization focuses on customer experience and return on investment (ROI) increases, so will investments across the organization.

Areas where you probably need to invest more are:

- Processes needed to map the Customer Life Cycle and correlate strategic objectives with marketing and digital objectives
- Contextualization (starting with the most important channels)
- Building the single view of the customer, connecting data from different repositories
- Actionable analytics

To find funds, you may need to reallocate your budgets. Some areas where you may want to reduce investment are:

- Broadcast or mass marketing (advertising and email blasts that are not targeted)
- Digital platforms that can be consolidated to integrate a limited number of channels
- Siloed marketing initiatives

BREAKING THROUGH THE BIGGEST BARRIERS TO MARKETING SUCCESS

To take the first step, it's important that you are willing and capable of breaking through some of the typical barriers to getting started. Remember, it's all about aligning people, process, and technology.

People

Changing the status quo from business as usual is not an easy task. Changing the marketing mind-set from launch-and-forget marketing to an agile, customer-centric and data-driven approach is a big change in mind-set. Like the rest of your life, you need great partners helping you along this journey. You need a mix of advocates, internal resources, and external resources that can bring together the know-how and guidance to start correctly. You need partners who are experienced and have done this type of work before.

Invest in people, first to make them realize the new opportunities at hand, and second to help them get started on this journey.

Process

If you want to build connected customer experiences that build lifetime customers, you must focus on using well-established processes that are battle tested. You don't want to blaze a new path and have to relearn best practices that are already proven.

Throughout this book, we provide different sets of processes, designed and presented to take your marketing competency to the next higher level. We provide examples, checklists, and frameworks that can be used as guidance to overcoming the process barrier.

Technology

Even though technology is the enabler of connected experiences, it can also be a barrier—especially with legacy platforms or too many platforms. The best way to start is by focusing on the customer touch points that are controlled through a connected platform. Typically these start with web, mobile, and email.

You should also consider the required speed to market, how the system will scale, how fast you can develop new skills, and your dependence on information technology (IT). While using the cloud for hosting your platform and data allows marketing to scale campaigns and rapidly launch new marketing initiatives, bear in mind they need to be deeply connected and not more silos of customer data.

There are many roads to take and many changes to make, but change is needed to connect with your customers, widen connection across channels, and create a connected experience.

We wrote this book to give you guidance on taking the first step toward the New Marketing Mandate. To help you on this exciting journey, we created a step-by-step Customer Experience Maturity Model that can be used as a road map and can help with the proper process.

Subsequent chapters describe the different stages of a Customer Experience Maturity Model, which highlight the issues you need to consider in each stage, with sections for people, process, technology, and barriers.

CHAPTER 3

Measuring Customer Experience Maturity

If you do not change direction, you may end up where you are heading.

—Lao Tzu

W hat can't be measured can't be managed. Your customers are using different devices and channels as part of their decision journey—gathering, analyzing, and deciding if they should engage with your brand. Customers increasingly expect that you recognize them, and continue the conversation where they left off in the last interaction.

From Chapter 1, we know that building connected experiences has great value for your customers. They get more relevant and personalized experiences, and for your organization it increases the chance of achieving your strategic objectives for your organization. In research conducted by Econsultancy,[1] 94 percent of organizations surveyed acknowledged that personalizing the experience will be critical for future success.

The problem is that 72 percent of marketers don't know how to start building these relevant, connected experiences using personalization.[2] They don't know what to do. And they don't know how to measure where they are to start, either.

That's very common among marketing organizations today, and it's something we have faced in our consulting with organizations across many industries.

This also led us to develop the Sitecore® Customer Experience Maturity Model™, as it's so easy to be overwhelmed with all the emerging technology and people and processes required. The maturity model allows you to take an incremental step at a time, building capability and value at each step.

TO BE SUCCESSFUL TAKES PEOPLE, PROCESS, AND TECHNOLOGY

Even if you have cutting-edge technology available to build the Amazon.coms of your market, you cannot succeed if you don't have the right people to add insights and creativity, and if those people don't have the processes to guide them. To succeed you need the people and processes to get the most value from the technology.

As a marketer you will always be on a never-ending journey because the destination, connecting with your customers, continually evolves. But if you are willing, and innovative, the farther you'll be able to go on this journey and the better you'll be able to connect to your customers and build lifetime advocacy. To help you on this journey, we have developed the Sitecore® Customer Experience Maturity Model™—a model with seven stages that maps the customer experience maturity level of your organization and offers guidance on how to evolve through the different stages of maturity. This is not an academic model. It is taken from years of experience and best practices earned by helping hundreds of organizations ranging from midsize to global enterprises.

The Customer Experience Maturity Model and the steps in this book are the process part of people, process, and technology. These processes can be applied to any organization using any leading connected platform for customer experience management.

CUSTOMER EXPERIENCE MATURITY MODEL

The maturity model focuses primarily on how to align your digital marketing efforts with marketing objectives that drive strategic objectives. These digital marketing efforts are what you use to impact customer experience at all your customer touch points and to ultimately achieve your strategic objectives. Creating compelling customer experiences requires an environment that reaches across your entire organization and impacts many teams that have contact with the customer, like call centers, points of sale, websites, mobile apps, and ancillary print material.

So even though we don't specifically cover call centers, points of sale, or other marketing vehicles, the model is still valid to improving your customer's experience and improving input to your teams and systems.

As your organization evolves to higher levels in the maturity model, the strategic value of marketing increases. (See Figure 3.1.) The model starts at the Initiate stage, a basic website, and grows to the seventh stage, the Lifetime Customers stage, where your organization and customer interactions use customer intelligence to predict patterns of behavior and connect with the most relevant content and calls to action, creating the best possible experience for the customer.

Our philosophy with regard to the Customer Experience Maturity Model is twofold:

1. If you want anything to last a lifetime, you have to care for it! The best way to care for customers is to go beyond just meeting their needs. You must anticipate their needs.

2. Anticipating customer needs is based on establishing a single view of the customer, using data collected from many touch points to make the customer's future experience more relevant so they not only feel more valued, but eventually become Lifetime Customers.

THREE PHASES IN THE CUSTOMER EXPERIENCE MATURITY MODEL

There are three macro phases that encompass the seven stages of the Customer Experience Maturity Model. These three phases are the overarching focus for the organization in building connected customer experiences:

1. Attract

2. Convert

3. Advocate

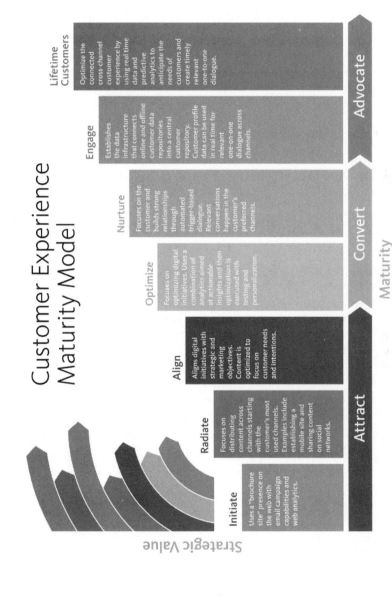

Customer Experience Maturity Model

Strategic Value

Initiate
Uses a "brochure site" presence on the web with email campaign capabilities and web analytics.

Radiate
Focuses on distributing content across channels starting with the customer's most used channels. Examples include establishing a mobile site and sharing content on social networks.

Align
Aligns digital initiatives with strategic and marketing objectives. Content is optimized to focus on customer needs and intentions.

Optimize
Focuses on optimizing digital initiatives. Uses a combination of analytics aimed at actionable insights and then optimization is executed with testing and personalization.

Nurture
Focuses on the customer and builds strong relationships through automated trigger-based dialogue. Relevant conversations happen in the customer's preferred channels.

Engage
Establishes the data infrastructure that connects online and offline customer data repositories into a central customer repository. Customer profile data can be used in real time for relevant one-on-one dialogue across channels.

Lifetime Customers
Optimize the connected cross-channel customer experience by using real time data and predictive analytics to anticipate the needs of customers and create timely relevant one-to-one dialogue.

Attract **Convert** **Advocate**

Maturity

Figure 3.1 Sitecore® Customer Experience Maturity Model™

In the Attract phase, organizations tend to focus on attracting more visitors through different channels. This is typically reflected by metrics for channels such as Visits and Likes. These key performance indicators (KPIs) aren't correlated to the organizations' strategic objectives and are difficult to relate to strategic objectives.

Organizations in the Attract phase tend to invest most of the marketing budget on attracting visitors instead of optimizing the experience and improving their relevance to visitors. This is not to suggest that spending to attract visitors is wrong, but the focus of the spending should be on what matters to your organization, which is like focusing only on maximizing the quantity of customers gained instead of also improving quality, in terms of profitability. The last stage of the Attract phase in the Customer Experience Maturity Model is the Align stage. In the Align stage organizations begin to align their digital goals and analytics with strategic and marketing objectives.

Based on our experience, aligning digital goals and marketing objectives with strategic objectives is essential. From the strategic standpoint, the purpose of marketing is to achieve strategic goals. From the day-to-day tactical standpoint, having clear strategic objectives makes it easier to track outcomes and to optimize marketing efforts.

In the Convert phase of the Customer Experience Maturity Model organizations focus on getting visitors committed and ultimately converting on key digital goals, those goals that are most likely to help achieve objectives. The focus here is converting by using various optimization tactics to provide better and more connected customer experiences. This can start with the low-hanging fruit of testing and personalization and then move to more advanced capabilities.

In the Advocate phase of the Customer Experience Maturity Model the focus is on creating strong advocates among customers. Advocates are customers that are more vocal. They recommend your brand and do more business with you. Research shows that promoters are 5.2 times more likely to buy more, compared to detractors.[3] Building customer advocates goes beyond marketing; it's an organizational task that involves different teams and systems. It takes the valuable customer insights from many teams and systems across many touch points to create customer advocates. Creating customers who are advocates is a critical competitive advantage.

STAGES IN THE CUSTOMER EXPERIENCE MATURITY MODEL

There are seven stages within the three phases of the Customer Experience Maturity Model. Each of these stages is an approach of people, process, and technology that marketing must evolve through to get to a higher level of customer experience. When you take the Customer Experience Maturity Assessment, referenced in the end of this chapter, you will learn what stage(s) your organization is currently in. In the following chapters you will read how your organization compares to others in your industry, learn about the specific details of each stage, and learn what steps your organization can take to move to higher levels. It's not only a vision of what your organization's future can be; it's a step-by-step guide on how to get there.

Initiate

The Initiate stage is the beginning of the customer experience journey. Most organizations at this stage have static websites. Marketers use email campaigns to send content to broadcast or to very large segments of recipients.

Most efforts go into creating and maintaining content that typically centers on the organization's point of view, not the customer's. Search engine optimization is key to attracting visitors to the site and has a heavy influence on which content is developed. The web analytics focus on site activity such as the number of visits or time on the site.

Value for Your Organization

The organization shares content about the organization, products, and services. This content gives generalized information to visitors and informs them of change with press releases or job postings.

Value for Your Customers

Customers have access to basic information about your organization and services as well as guidance on how to contact you.

KPIs

Traditional web analytics focus on traffic and content usage.

Tactics

Content is created and maintained from the organization's viewpoint. Search engine optimization is key to attracting visitors, and influences which content is needed. Email is used to broadcast content to customers.

Radiate

In the Radiate stage, organizations begin reaching out to customers through multiple channels, not just mass email. The organization develops a mobile website and begins building a social presence. Marketing recognizes that the customer comes first, knows which channels the customer uses, and distributes content through those channels. As content becomes more accessible through different channels, it reaches more customers in the context the customer expects and uses. Customers, especially through social channels, are much more likely to share marketing's content with others and broaden the distribution and connections. Analytics focus on channel volume and effectiveness. Connection through customer-centric channels is a key objective for organizations in the radiate stage. Pay-per-click (PPC) programs grow as a method of attracting more customers, and give insights into intent of the customers.

Value for Your Organization

Content distribution begins to go through specific channels used by customers. Content focus becomes more on brand and increases the likeliness of customers including you as part of their decision journey and thereby increases the potential to reach larger audiences.

Value for Your Customers

Content is accessible through multiple channels, making it easier for customers to research and find your information. By connecting channels and giving your customers the ability to share content with their peers, you increase your distribution and your content becomes more relevant.

KPIs

Traditional web analytics continues to be used but with greater awareness of channel performance and segmentation.

Tactics

Context begins to form content, with mobile and social channels changing the content, style, and layout. Integrating messages across channels is more prevalent, giving a single message to customers. Customers share and like content on web and mobile sites.

Align

In the Align stage, executives and marketers begin to ask, "Why does our website exist?" "Why do we have five people working on creating content for social channels?" "Why did we just spend $1 million on a new mobile app?"

Key to answering these questions is aligning digital goals with marketing objectives that drive strategic objectives; an important focus at this stage is on achieving well-defined marketing objectives. Customer information provides a more informed view to marketing and sales about customer needs and intent.

Value for Your Organization

As marketing aligns with business objectives, reports show executives how marketing is driving business, where optimization is needed, and where additional investments are needed.

Value for Your Customers

Marketing realizes that it needs better and more relevant content that helps customers through the decision journey. Typically this changes the nature of the content so that content becomes more customer-centric.

KPIs

Experience Analytics complement traditional analytics. Value and Value per Visit are used to compare and optimize across different channels. Management and executive reports focus on marketing's impact on business objectives.

Tactics

Analytics focuses on business outcomes, the effectiveness of marketing, and the quality of customers. Marketers compare cross-channel effectiveness and make holistic decisions looking at the entire cross-channel portfolio, moving away from optimizing individual silos. Campaigns are leveraged or optimized using the Marketing Optimization Matrix discussed in Chapter 7, which considers both value and attractiveness.

Optimize

In the Optimize stage, marketers focus on improving key customer touch points, starting with the most important digital channels used by the customers. Marketers also focus on making the customer experience more relevant to customers' needs and intent. With the focus on customer relevance, there is more monitoring and optimizing of content and channels as a way of achieving business objectives. Customer profiles are built, and content is mapped to personas or customer segments and the decision journey. Personalization tailors content to increase relevance to specific segments.

Value for Your Organization

The Optimize stage focuses on accelerating customers through the decision journey and converting on key digital goals that drive marketing and strategic objectives.

Value for Your Customers

Marketing becomes more relevant as content, messages, and channels are optimized to achieve high value, which in turn makes all marketing efforts more relevant to customers. This is a win-win for customers and marketers.

KPIs

Marketing's targets and metrics align with the organization's strategic objectives. Marketing can prove its effectiveness, and it is easier to justify new initiatives and additional resources.

Tactics

Simple personalization increases the relevance for customers, as they see content that is more relevant to their needs. A/B testing increases conversion rates and identifies content that is more relevant.

New initiatives in tracking customer behavior builds customer-related data and profiling for use in personas. Customer communities are built to increase sharing and distribution to peers.

Nurture

The Nurture stage uses more advanced optimization capabilities to enhance the customer experience and increase total conversions. Nurturing increases customer engagement and provides a cross-channel dialogue with the customer based on the customer's profile. At this stage organizations initiate automated marketing flows mapped to stages of the customer decision journey as well as the entire Customer Life Cycle. For example, a customer might first connect with marketing due to a thought leadership paper during the early stages of the decision journey. This could be followed by nurturing sequences about the best use of products or services that accelerate the customer through the decision journey.

Value for Your Organization

Marketing and sales teams are given an extra level of power and credibility with customers due to the nurturing programs customers have received. Customers are more accepting and informed when they first make contact with sales.

Automated two-way dialogue with customers informs the organization about customer intent and usage of products and services.

Value for Your Customers

Based on their behavior, customers are able to get valuable information relevant to their intent for that stage in the decision journey.

KPIs

Metrics include information about activity and engagement at different stages in the decision journey. Conversion funnels may map micro and macro conversion goals.

Tactics

Focus is on relevant customer-centric dialogue, which is based on collecting explicit and implicit information about the customer that can be used as a basis for the automated flows.

Social channels are more integrated, and behavior can be captured from these channels and used to enrich the customer profile.

Engage

This stage can be a huge step for many organizations, as Engage focuses on connecting the different customer data repositories—it empowers a single view of the customer across online and offline touch points. In many cases, creating this is a transformational task, as it includes data from many repositories and crosses different organizational units. But building this repository is necessary in order to be relevant to the customer at any time and at any touch point. It is also necessary for all units in the organization to have a single, integrated view of the customer. You need this single view to collect behavior and data from all channels and have those data accessible in real time at any customer touch point.

Value for Your Organization

For organizations that succeed in building the single view of the customer, the value is tremendous; not only are they able to build relevant connected experiences in the different touch points, but they also enrich the data across different organizational units. Salespeople get access to all customer data, making for better customer conversations. Marketing gets better data for segmentation and personalization, which results in more focused marketing efforts.

Value for Your Customers

Customers feel more valued and even positively surprised when they receive messages that are relevant at each touch point with the organization.

KPIs

Targets and metrics are tied to a Customer Life Cycle funnel using customer-level metrics segmented for specific channels.

Tactics

Customer data is connected to give a single view of the customer so that a picture of the customer is available at any touch point along the decision journey.

Calls to action are automated based on similar behavior from other customers.

Lifetime Customers

At this stage the organization uses customer insights blended with intelligence, predictions, and agility as a key competitive advantage. Customer intelligence and predictive algorithms optimize the customer experience across multiple channels. Agility is key, and the speed of launching or testing new initiatives becomes a competitive advantage. The organization not only anticipates the needs of the customer, but also uses predictive analytics to launch initiatives in anticipation of a customer's needs. Automated big data analysis keeps the organization informed and able to react quickly with data-driven decisions.

Value for Your Organization

Data drives decisions in achieving marketing and strategic objectives. Optimizing efficiency and effectiveness drives organizational units.

Value for Your Customers

Not only is content relevant, but it also gives great value to customers by providing recommendations that are timely and closely matched to their needs.

KPIs

Targets and metrics are closely tied to deeper and more detailed decision journeys, and forecast future outcomes. Customer Lifetime Value (CLV) is used with loyalty and retention.

Tactics

Data is used at every level to make every touch point immediate, relevant, and predictive.

Automated data analysis provides actionable advice for optimization across most digital areas.

Cross-channel attribution optimizes marketing initiatives.

Predictive analytics informs executives on probable future outcomes.

The seven stages of the Customer Experience Maturity Model are covered in greater detail in Chapters 6 through 11.

MAPPING TO CAPABILITIES

When you know which maturity stage you are in, it's best to first build a solid foundation of technology and capabilities. This will make your move to the next higher level easier and safer.

The version of the Customer Experience Maturity Model presented in Figure 3.2 shows technical capabilities mapped to the different stages and how they progress.

For instance, social sharing starts as part of the Radiate stage, helping you distribute content on social channels. As you move across to the Align stage, social listening is used to monitor the alignment between customer relevance and achieving organizational objectives. During the Nurture stage you will want to use social channels to engage your customers individually.

Another example is testing. Testing starts with simple A/B testing as part of the Optimize stage. As the benefits and value of testing are recognized, you will invest more in testing and begin using more advanced testing like multivariate testing in the Nurture stage.

CRAWL, WALK, RUN, FLY!

Based on our extensive analysis on the maturity of different organizations, covered in the next chapter, we see that the majority of organizations are in the first two of seven stages. Therefore, we strongly recommend that for most organizations their first action should be to use the current stage to build a mobile presence and create social connections that radiate out to customers. Following that, a key task will be aligning strategic objectives, marketing objectives, and digital goals—doing this will ensure that your marketing foundation is stable and is based on achieving your organization's objectives.

In the short term, many organizations will want to prove their business case, harvesting the low-hanging fruit as described in Stage 4,

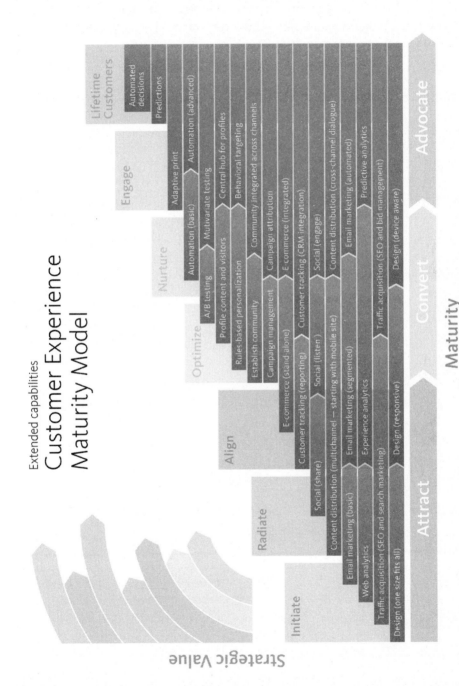

Figure 3.2 Sitecore® Customer Experience Maturity Model™ with Capabilities

Optimize. In the longer term, the ambition should be moving to the higher stages while coordinating maturity across your entire organization so that silos don't develop.

NEXT STEPS: HOW MATURE IS YOUR ORGANIZATION?

An important part of any journey is understanding where you currently are, so you can properly map your destination. To help with this, we've created a tool to assess how mature your organization is, measure where you are today so you can establish a baseline, and then use this book to help guide your progress.

Visit www.ConnectTheExperience.com/cxassessment and fill in the assessment. Once you have completed it and received the evaluation of your organization's maturity, continue to the next chapter and learn how you compare with others in your industry.

NOTES

1. "The Realities of Online Personalization," Econsultancy.com Ltd., April 2013.
2. IBID for the 72 percent.
3. "The State of Customer Experience (CX) Infographics," Temkin Group, 2013.

CHAPTER 4

How Does Your Organization Compare?

The best vision is insight.

—Malcolm Forbes

With more than 1,000 participants in our Customer Experience Maturity Assessment, we have gathered many insights on marketing maturity across industries and how marketing organizations use new technology capabilities, as well as their organizational maturity. What we found shocked us. Those marketing organizations that take advantage of these findings have the opportunity to leapfrog their competition.

THE TIME FOR CHANGE IS NOW

For too many years, too many marketing organizations have watched the digital transformation happening right outside their door. But they have not taken an active role in embracing technology, building knowledge, increasing staff that would help them move into data-driven marketing, or simply taking advantage of new technology to win market share.

Considering that we are at the beginning of a revolution, the findings from our research are scary. Our analysis shows that 85.4 percent of organizations are at the very beginning levels of customer experience maturity. They are in either the Initiate stage (67 percent) or the Radiate stage (18.4 percent), as shown in Figure 4.1. For many organizations, that means they need to focus on using their

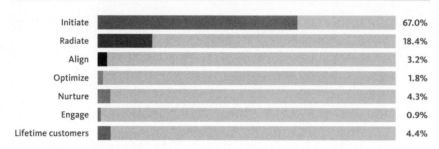

Figure 4.1   Customer Experience Maturity Level

current stage to distribute content through the channels most used by customers and then move up to the next stage, Align. In the Align stage organizations align their digital goals to drive marketing objectives that achieve strategic objectives. It is data-driven marketing that achieves business objectives.

BIGGEST BARRIER TO MARKETING MATURITY

When doing our research and analysis, we found that the biggest barrier for entering the higher levels of maturity is how current technology is being used today!

For large organizations that use many technologies, the marketing data and technology actually span many different departments; for example:

- Marketing owns web content management and testing.

- Business intelligence owns analytics.

- Public relations owns social.

- Customer relationship management owns email marketing and marketing automation.

- Sales owns offline conversations.

With this landscape filled with silos, your organization will have different teams connecting with the customer at different touch points and providing different content. And each team is in a different context (the environment and device used by the customer).

This fragmentation of systems is at the heart of the biggest issue today, and is what prevents customers from having a connected, relevant experience. To deliver the connected experience organizations should have connected systems that need to work from a single view of the customer and have data collected across all the touch points accessible in real time. From this single view, marketing can build a coherent and relevant conversation in real time. To do that, the organization with the widest use of technology needs to either integrate systems or establish a customer data hub containing the single view of the customer. That hub needs to update in real time.

The first option, creating a single integrated system, is a big task. Creating such a system is not easy. It usually requires custom development that integrates data across multiple systems, is constantly updated, and maintains a single system of record that can drive events and actions across systems (see Figure 4.2).

Creating a customer data hub, the second option is more feasible, but this also requires custom development. You need to have a real-time integration to the data hub with the single view of the customer, which is actionable. If you are an organization with few data repositories, this is more straightforward; however, for organizations with many data repositories, this is not an easy task as they are owned by different business units.

The best option if you are starting from scratch is to have one connected platform, which builds on a single view of the customer and allows you to own the experience in the different channels used by the customer, because it brings together customer data with the interactions and experiences being delivered to the customer.

This is also the approach that many start-up business disrupters use. To remain agile, they don't rely on legacy systems or separate data repositories; instead they start building data systems from scratch with the single view of the customer in mind. Their future view is to be more relevant to their customers than their competitors are.

How Do You Compare to Your Industry?

We segmented the survey results by industry and found roughly the same pattern: most organizations are at Initiate or Radiate (see Figure 4.3). These Stage 1 and Stage 2 organizations should focus

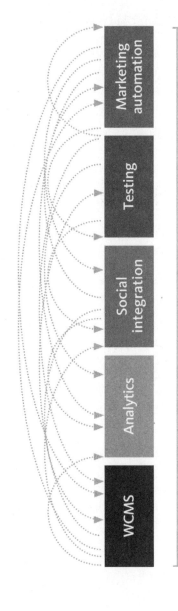

Single view of the customer?

Figure 4.2 Complexity by Integrating Five Systems

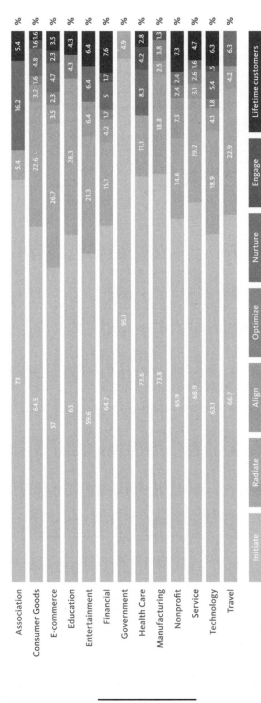

Figure 4.3 Across Industries, Most Organizations Remain in the Earliest Stages

first on getting the full benefits of Radiate before going to the Align stage, and then focus on optimizing the customer experience as well as the organizational outcome.

When looking at maturity across industries, even though most are in the early stages, it's worth noticing that the majority of industries have a few organizations that are very mature. With the exception of government and travel, all industries have a few organizations at the highest maturity levels, Engage or Lifetime Customers. Looking at only the top stages, the financial services sector is the most mature and government is the farthest behind.

For additional information on specific industries, go to the companion website for this book at www.ConnectTheExperience.com/cxassessment. You can take the assessment and get benchmark data for your industry.

HOW DO WE MEASURE SUCCESS?

Many websites have not evolved beyond using first-generation legacy web analytics such as visits, page views, time on site, and so on. We found that 43 percent of organizations either don't measure (14.9 percent) or only use visits (28.1 percent) to report on digital success (see Figure 4.4). Forty-three percent is a huge percentage still using an ineffective metric. There is a big need for measuring the impact of digital success on strategic objectives.

The second highest measure of success is conversions with 24.1 percent of organizations using that metric. Only 22.8 percent have digital key performance indicators (KPIs) aligned with strategic

Does not specifically measure digital success	14.9%
Visits	28.1%
Conversions	24.1%
KPI's aligned with business objectives	22.8%
KPI's aligned with customer lifecycle	10.1%

Figure 4.4   How Organizations Measure Success across Digital Channels

business objectives, and 10.1 percent have digital KPIs aligned with Customer Life Cycle (CLC) across both online and offline channels. Only slightly more than 30 percent of organizations have a metric they feel relates to a business objective. There is certainly opportunity for improvement.

How Does Your Top-Level Management Compare for Involvement with Digital Strategy?

To gain the greatest value from digital marketing and digital strategy, it must become an intrinsic part of the organization. Digital marketing becomes marketing. Digital strategy becomes strategy. To make this happen requires an executive-sponsored mandate requiring collaboration among many departments.

Our research shows that only 29 percent of organizations have the backup they need with high involvement from top-level executives, while 30.3 percent have medium involvement, 31.4 percent have low involvement, and 9.2 percent have no involvement (see Figure 4.5).

Not involved	9.2%
Low involvement	31.4%
Medium involvement	30.3%
High involvement	29.0%

Figure 4.5 **How Top-Level Managers Are Involved with Digital Strategy**

How Do You Compare in Optimizing for Mobile Devices?

Organizations must adapt to customers' increasing use of mobile devices at different stages in their journeys and beyond. A few of the facts on this major change in how customers access the web include:

- Estimates show that by 2015 there will be more people using mobile than desktop to access the Internet.[1]

- During Cyber Monday 2013, mobile share of sales was 17 percent.[2]

If you haven't optimized for mobile devices, you are most likely missing opportunities.

Our research shows that 48 percent of organizations have optimized for mobile, leaving 52 percent needing to prioritize for mobile users. Having sites that are optimized for mobile devices is an important part of moving into the Radiate stage and provides great potential for increasing business outcome, as we describe in Chapter 6.

E-commerce is leading the shift to mobile with 62 percent having optimized for mobile devices, whereas government is lagging behind with only 29 percent that have optimized for mobile devices.

How Do You Compare in Using Segmented Email Campaigns?

Many email campaigns are "send and forget" campaigns. Marketers with this attitude look only at metrics like open and click-through rates. However, having data about your customers and email recipients means you can take a more strategic approach to email. That approach more typically comes as part of Stage 3, Align. In the Align stage you want to utilize data for email segmentation so you can be more relevant in your campaigning and avoid irrelevant and untimely content.

Fifty-two percent of respondents said they are using data available on email recipients to do simple segmentation of email. Once an organization has a strategic focus, it measures email campaigns by the email's effectiveness on business metrics, such as value produced, rather than opens or click-through rates. The leader in using email segmentation is travel with 67 percent; government trails with 24 percent.

How Do You Compare in Using Testing to Optimize Customer Experience?

Testing is great for going from guesswork to actual feedback from customers consuming your content. Testing is a well-proven tactic to increase conversions. Forrester Research found that 96 percent of organizations using testing increased conversions by 1 percent or more, and 77 percent faced increased conversions by 6 percent or more.[3]

We found that 29 percent of organizations use A/B split testing or multivariate (MV) testing to increase outcome, which leaves 71 percent guessing at how they can optimize the experience. A/B and multivariate testing is a prime optimization technique that is being ignored.

Testing is an established practice with e-commerce, which is leading with 44 percent. Government lags behind with only 17 percent using testing.

How Do You Compare in Using Personalization to Be More Relevant?

Personalization can have a great impact on increasing outcome. Research has found that organizations that are using personalization to optimize the website experience are seeing, on average, a 19 percent uplift in sales.[4]

We found that personalization is used by 29 percent of organizations. Focusing on the low-hanging fruit of personalization is a great start for going into the Optimize stage, and with the significant impact it could have on conversions, this is a not-to-be-missed opportunity.

The leader sector in personalization is associations with 43 percent. Government lags with 17 percent.

How Do You Compare in Using Behavioral Targeting to Adapt to Visitor Browsing?

A more advanced form of optimization is to use implicit visitor browsing to personalize and display relevant content; 23 percent of organizations use this to optimize customer interactions online and the connected experience that will help them climb to the Nurture stage.

The leader in behavioral targeting, again, is associations with 38 percent. Government lags with 15 percent.

How Do You Compare to Organizations Using Marketing Automation?

Marketing automation is well established and broadly used to nurture prospects to become customers, to help with onboarding, or in upsell and recapture programs.

Several studies show that nurture programs using marketing automation improve business outcomes.

Currently, 29 percent of the organizations surveyed are using marketing automation. Entertainment is the leading industry with 45 percent, and nonprofit lags with 22 percent.

How Do You Compare to Those Having a Single View of the Customer across Online and Offline Touch Points?

The high value produced by multichannel marketing is apparent when 40 percent of those surveyed reported an increase of more than 15 percent in marketing-attributed revenue and 60 percent reported a 10 percent increase in Return on Marketing Investment (ROMI).[5] This was attributed to having a single view of the customer across different touch points. This single view was used to optimize the conversation and the connected experience. This is an essential part of the Engage stage.

Currently 30 percent of organizations have a single view of the customer, with e-commerce leading with 47 percent and government lagging with only 12 percent.

When we followed up with organizations to understand the functionality of their single view of the customer, we found that very few had the capability to create real-time personalization using that data, which is a core element in creating connected experiences.

How Do You Compare in Using Predictive Analytics to Steer Content Targeting for Specific Customers?

Predictive analytics is crucial in making the right decisions and automating decisions that drive the conversations needed in the Lifetime Customers stage.

Instead of looking at the past, predictive analytics will help organizations be more relevant and anticipate the next best action for their customers. Currently 21 percent of organizations are using predictive analytics, with entertainment leading with 34 percent and government lagging with only 10 percent.

Get the Sitecore Customer Experience Maturity Assessment Benchmark at www.ConnectTheExperience.com/cxbenchmark.

MAPPING PEOPLE, PROCESS, AND TECHNOLOGY TO THE CUSTOMER EXPERIENCE MATURITY MODEL

To better understand gaps among people, process, and technology in the stages of the maturity model, we analyzed survey data to gain additional insights.

We took the main phases of the Customer Experience Maturity Model—Attract, Convert, and Advocate—and for each phase we mapped the people, process, and technology requirement for that phase. If organizations met all requirements, they would get 100 percent in people, 100 percent in process, and 100 percent in technology.

Technology

For the three phases, we looked primarily at:

1. *Attract.* Technology to support distribution content in different channels and web analytics

2. *Convert.* Technology to support optimization such as testing, personalization, and marketing automation, as well as being able to collect customer intelligence at the different touch points

3. *Advocate.* Technology to support predictions and automate relevant content across channels, as well as having the single view of the customer

For the Attract phase, we found that approximately half of the organizations have the right technology in place to distribute content in the primary channels used by customers, web, mobile, social, and email, as well as having established basic web analytics (see Figure 4.6).

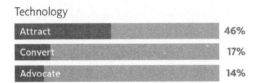

Figure 4.6   **Technology Usage in Attract, Convert, and Advocate Phases**

In the Convert phase, only 17 percent have technology in place to optimize the experience and to focus on converting the visitor to a customer. Technology here is mostly dominated by adoption of testing, with advanced personalization being underutilized. Fourteen percent of organizations have the needed technology for the Advocate phase, dominated by those organizations having the single view in place. But even those organizations lack using that data for predictions as well as real-time automated optimization.

To better understand how technology is used for multichannel marketing and analytics, we analyzed on these two aspects alone across the three phases (see Figure 4.7).

Even though both of these areas are important uses of technology, they are underutilized. Technology use here should be a short-term priority for those organizations that don't yet have it in place. At the Attract phase, 54 percent have analytics in place with proper insights, but only 43 percent are able to use channels preferred by their

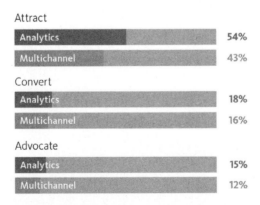

Figure 4.7   **Multichannel Marketing and Analytics Adoption in Attract, Convert, and Advocate Phases**

customers—with nearly half having a mobile presence, 54 percent using email marketing, and 34.5 percent having social integration.

In the Convert and Advocate phases, many organizations don't have the technology for first using insights to optimize the experience in a preferred channel and later for using predictions and automation to do this at scale.

People

For the three phases, we looked primarily at:

- *Attract.* Having marketers, digital analysts, and acquisition marketers

- *Convert.* Having channel experts and optimization experts

- *Advocate.* Having data analysts and a chief digital officer or chief marketing technologist

Figure 4.8 shows that staffing is most mature in the Attract phase, but has serious limitations in all phases.

It surprised us that half of the organizations have data analysts, but in most cases that role is currently within another team. In the future this could be an important asset to shift to marketing. Only 5 percent have a chief digital officer or a chief marketing technologist. Looking at the Attract phase, just below a third of the organizations have digital analysts and fewer have acquisition marketers. In the Convert phase, less than half have channel experts and only 25 percent have optimization experts.

Looking at barriers that are preventing organizations from reaching high maturity, lack of the correct staff is one of the most dominant.

Chapter 12 has more details on the specific roles and skills as organizations move up the Customer Experience Maturity Model.

Figure 4.8   People in Attract, Convert, and Advocate Phases

Process

For the three phases we looked at:

1. *Attract*: Having processes in place to gather data and use that for channel optimization

2. *Convert*: Having processes that support gathering customer data that will enrich the experience across the different channels

3. *Advocate*: Having processes that support the use of automation based on data, and use data for predictions, either customer focused or input to organizational financial budgets

A big barrier to a connected customer experience is having the processes to support getting the most value out of technology and resources. In Figure 4.9 we see a big gap where only 27 percent of organizations have the needed processes in place for the Attract phase and only 10 percent for the Convert and Advocate phases.

Figure 4.9   Process Support in Attract, Convert, and Advocate Phases

Figure 4.10 looks at people, process, and technology within the three phases.

It's clear that organizations need to invest in the right processes, as this is currently the biggest gap.

WHERE ARE ORGANIZATIONS INVESTING?

Many organizations understand the potential for using technology to create better-connected experiences. In the area of near-term technology investments, mobile tops the list, as shown in Figure 4.11.

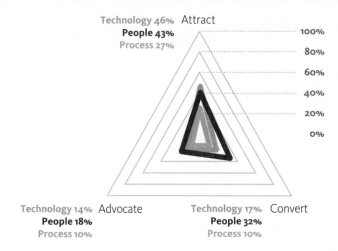

Technology 46% Attract
People 43%
Process 27%

100%
80%
60%
40%
20%
0%

Technology 14% Advocate
People 18%
Process 10%

Technology 17% Convert
People 32%
Process 10%

Figure 4.10 People, Process, and Technology Mapped in Attract, Convert, and Advocate Phases

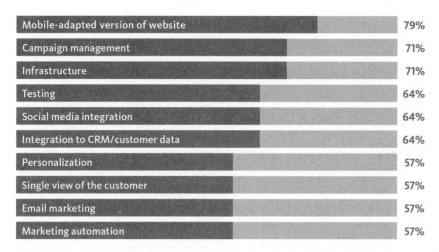

Mobile-adapted version of website	79%
Campaign management	71%
Infrastructure	71%
Testing	64%
Social media integration	64%
Integration to CRM/customer data	64%
Personalization	57%
Single view of the customer	57%
Email marketing	57%
Marketing automation	57%

Figure 4.11 Technology Investments

One concern is that organizations that have realized that they have fallen behind tend to invest in short-term capabilities. In reality, all of these areas need to be aligned to give the greatest impact so they are helping with the connected experience and focusing on the customers. However, the risk in focusing on many investments at the same time is that the focus gets diluted.

When we surveyed organizations about what would give the most value in the short term, web analytics, email marketing, and

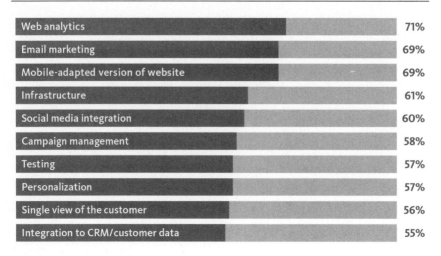

Figure 4.12 Short-Term Value Gain

a mobile-adapted version of the website top the list, as shown in Figure 4.12. All of these are part of the Attract phase.

WHAT MUST YOU DO?

So what must you do if you aren't the industry leader? What if your marketing is in the early stages of maturity?

To quote Robert Frost, "The best way out is through it." You literally need to get on the train instead of watching it pull away from you and get started now. You need to make the decision, jump on board, and start building the next-generation marketing machine.

To start with, look at your success metrics for digital marketing. Are you looking at visits and page views instead of KPIs aligned with business objectives? If you are, then you need to align and rework your marketing to take advantage of the power of digital channels. You need to look at your customers, their journeys, their motives, their intents, and the touch points where you connect. You need a map to show you how to create an active, engaging conversation with your customers. To do that you need to own the experience across the channels your customers prefer. This will take investment, but it's necessary to build your marketing organization's experience, skills, and knowledge so you can move to higher levels of marketing maturity.

You may be trapped in an organization where business units own functional silos. Each silo controls different parts of the customer journey as well as the data for that silo. If you are surrounded by silos, then the best approach might be to gather allies and move forward with a business case that shows how the entire organization will benefit. Chapter 5, Making It Happen!, describes some proven techniques for creating change in small and large organizations.

If you're finding it difficult to make change happen and get an executive sponsor, get started by using the information from the Customer Experience Maturity Assessment to see where you can get ahead of your competitors. Let's take one of the easiest examples, one that will significantly improve most organizations. With 85.4 percent of organizations in Stage 1 and Stage 2, there are a few steps almost any organization can take to jump ahead. For example:

1. Are you among the 52 percent that don't yet have a mobile presence? If so, then adding mobile is a great place to fill the gap between your customers' use of mobile and your lack of having mobile.

2. Are you part of the 71 percent of marketers who don't test the experience? Begin using A/B split testing to find out what really works.

3. Are you among the 48 percent that don't use email marketing segmentation? A quick win would be looking at data and starting to segment recipients so content is more relevant.

4. Are your customers using social, but you are among the 65.5 percent that don't have social integration? Perhaps you should explore what social could add to your customers' experience.

5. Are you writing content for a specific visitor segment and stage? If you are guilty of random acts of marketing, then create a Digital Relevancy Map and use it to focus your content on key visitor segments and specific stages in their decision journeys.

6. Are you among the 67 percent of organizations that can't tie their KPIs to strategic and marketing objectives? Move into the Align stage by mapping how digital goals drive

marketing objectives, and then create and implement an Engagement Value Scale. Even if you put an Engagement Value on only your most important digital goal, you'll be able to track which channels, campaigns, pages, and assets have the greatest impact.

With these six steps that almost any organization can implement, you should jump ahead of the majority of your industry.

Every Industry Has a Customer Experience Leader

Anyone who has been awake in the past 10 years has seen the shifting of business continents. Amazon.com's rise has pushed Barnes & Noble into a corner and has crushed Borders into extinction. Netflix, a business model that some scoffed at, has smothered Blockbuster. The list goes on.

What we are seeing is an evolutionary change that is probably the biggest in mercantile history. But this change where a few dominate the majority isn't new. It's just happening faster, and the rise of marketing using technology is allowing it to happen across many industries and business models. It won't happen just in B2B or B2C. This change is happening in nonprofits, in services, in online education, and in all forms of people-to-people connection touched by the Internet.

The change is happening now. As our assessments of more than 1,000 organizations show, 85.4 percent of organizations are still in Stages 1 and 2 of the seven stages of customer experience maturity. If you ranked in Stage 1 or Stage 2, you might think you can feel comfortable being there with the vast majority. But that is a false sense of security. In most of the industry segments surveyed there was at least one organization in Stage 7.

If You Aren't at the Top, Where Does That Leave You?

Michael Porter is recognized around the world as the father of competitive analysis. His groundbreaking work in the evolution of industries has revealing insights that marketers need to consider to be customer-centric. The tectonic shifts caused by technology have been seen before, and we can learn from them.

Most business professionals in fast-changing industries are familiar with the Rogers' bell curve known as the "adoption curve." The adoption curve shows how buyers of new products and services begin with a few innovators, then come the early adopters, and so forth, creating a familiar bell-shape curve.

At the beginning of the adoption curve there is shallow growth as only a few innovators purchase new products. Gradually more buy until the curve becomes like a bulge in a python. Following the bulge come the late adopters, the last to buy.

What Porter discovered is what happens to the companies behind the customer adoption curve. (Porter studied industries like railroads and appliances, but I think you'll see how this applies to all industries.) From his studies that examined many industries, he found that during the first part of the adoption curve there was a high growth in companies providing products or services to that area. Those of us familiar with Silicon Valley know this as the "hockey stick" growth curve.

At the middle of the adoption curve, where the bulge is, the market is saturated by sometimes hundreds of companies supplying almost the same product or service. As the market becomes saturated and only late adopters are left, there is a vast number of mediocre companies stuck in the middle. Most are undifferentiated and have a sliver of market share. As the adoption curve becomes mature and shallow, there is only enough room for a few large companies. The large companies swallow up high-quality smaller ones and the lower-quality players disappear.

This gruesome evolutionary curve has repeated over and over across many industries for more than 100 years. Now we are faced with a similar situation in marketing. The marketing leaders who create the best customer experiences and grab the largest volume of customer advocates will be the survivors.

Making Your Choice

So what do you do? There are only a limited number of choices, but the good thing is that there is still time to make a winning choice and execute it well. However, given the past, you probably have less than two or three years to make your choice. Technology adoption history shows that change happens slowly, but when it hits the inflection point (the tipping point) the rate of change explodes.

Here are three choices for your future:

1. *Do nothing.* Keep your marketing organization with the 85.4 percent that are currently in Stage 1 or Stage 2. The problem with this choice is that you will be left behind. Your marketing power will diminish and it will be incredibly difficult to catch up. Just ask newspaper publishers. They saw the future of the Internet coming in the 1990s, yet failed to adapt to the Internet.

2. *Grab a profitable niche and own it and the customers.* In the studies of how industries evolve there are only two or three companies that rise to the top of an industry. The rest are acquired, merge, or die. However, at the opposite end from the large dominant companies are a few small companies that completely control a niche market. So one winning strategy is to find a profitable niche you can dominate using customer intimacy as one of your strategic themes. Use technology to engage totally with your customers by knowing everything about the customer, becoming an icon in their culture, and serving their niche needs.

3. *Accelerate and dominate.* As companies fight their way out of the maelstrom in the middle, two or three rise to the top. One dominates, but the other one or two are still viable and have respectable large businesses. If you are going to become one of these top organizations, you must begin now to grow your (digital) marketing expertise and technology.

This shift will accelerate. The next few years will see the advent of cloud-based marketing using big data analytics. At that point those that have a large market share will be extremely difficult if not impossible to catch up to. They will not just engage customers; they will predict customer needs and make recommendations before the customer is consciously aware of the need.

NOTES

1. "The Mobile Internet Report," Morgan Stanley Research, 2010.
2. "Cyber Monday Report 2013," IBM, December 2013.
3. "The State of Online Testing 2011," Forrester Research.
4. "The Realities of Online Personalization," Econsultancy.com Ltd., April 2013.
5. "The Multichannel Maturity Mandate," Forrester Research, May 2012.

CHAPTER 5

Making It Happen!

The brick walls are there for a reason. The brick walls are not there to keep us out. The brick walls are there to give us a chance to show how badly we want something.

—Randy Pausch, *The Last Lecture*

W e've all heard the mantra, "What gets measured gets managed." It sounds so simple to manage a change project. The problem is that just because you're managing something doesn't mean it will happen. There's a lot that needs to be coordinated and changed. There's a lot of inertia. And there's a lot of attitude.

WHAT BARRIERS ARE PREVENTING YOU FROM MATURING?

In many years of consulting, speaking at conferences, hosting forums, and talking with chief marketing officers (CMOs) and digital strategists, one question always sparks an emotional discussion: "What barriers are preventing you from achieving a higher level of customer experience maturity?"

Our research with the Customer Experience Maturity Model reinforced the casual tally of responses we had kept over years of the top barriers that prevent organizations from maturing. You can see in Chapter 4 where process is one of the biggest gaps:

- Lack of resources

- Lack of budget

- Uncertainty in process or direction
- Lack of capability in existing technology
- Lack of executive support or buy-in
- Lack of clear understanding of return on investment
- Difficulty recruiting staff
- Difficulty retaining staff

Some of these barriers have the same root cause. For example, having a clear understanding of process and strategic direction gives focus, which reduces the need for resources. Also, having a clear understanding of the business case will create a clear Return on Marketing Investment (ROMI). That will give you executive buy-in, which in turn cures a lot of ills.

Once you have a clear direction and clarity on processes, the rest of these barriers are ones you can scale.

STEPS TO SUCCESSFULLY IMPROVE MARKETING

You can have the right metrics, beautiful charts and dashboards, great management style, and even motivated teams, but still projects and improvement efforts fail. In fact, organizations have incredibly high failure rates when they attempt to make large changes or take on large projects. Why?

The failure rate is high usually not because of technical skills or tools. Rather it's because of people, process, and organizational inertia. Just like in physics, things tend to remain the same. Unless you have *great* processes and motivated people, the organization will return to its original position or speed.

We want to show you two complementary ways you can approach changing the people and processes in your organization. Each has a metaphor behind it that's easy to remember. The first is the Burning Platform. The second is the Trapeze Theory.

The Burning Platform is one of the most common ways of changing an organization. It depends on scaring the heck out of people: "Either we change or we all die." As you might expect, it can highly motivate the right team of people, can demotivate others, discredit management if it's not true, and in almost all cases has a high failure rate.

The Trapeze Theory of change is a method of helping the people in organizations move from an old platform to a new platform. It is a model that helps managers think about how to motivate the movement from the old platform, support people during transition, and reward them for staying on the new platform. In past work helping large organizations transition from legacy to new computer systems the Trapeze Theory of change has helped managers understand how they can make the change easier, faster, and ensure that the change "sticks."

The Trapeze Theory gives people a solid foundation of confidence, doesn't disrupt your organization as much, and has a high success rate. It's based on good, humane management skills.

Each of these methods is useful in different types of organizations, with different cultures, and in different change environments. You need to know which one to use for each situation you face. It's best to keep your tool kit stocked with different options and pick the tool that's best for the job.

Let's first examine the Burning Platform method, also known as "change or die." A later section describes the Trapeze Theory.

Burning Platform Method of Organizational Change

The first and one of the most widely used models for organizational change is often referred to as the Burning Platform. The metaphor came from Daryl Conner. Conner relates that he had been researching how executives behave when their organization had to change to survive. (Notice the "change or die" situation.)

One evening in 1988 Conner was watching television when he saw a horrific story of the Piper Alpha oil-drilling platform high above the freezing North Sea off the coast of Scotland. The platform had exploded and caught fire. The workers were taught not to jump, as the fall of 15 stories and the freezing water were certain death; in fact, the explosion, fire, and bitter elements caused the deaths of 165 crew members and two rescuers.

Of the 61 who survived, Andy Mochan, a superintendent, lived by jumping from the high platform into the freezing water filled with floating debris. When interviewed later, Andy said, "It was either jump or fry."

That is the same feeling that many executives have in using this Burning Platform model of organizational change. The executives and professionals who use a Burning Platform model for change must really be faced with a "do or die" situation.

Conner went on to write *Leading at the Edge of Chaos: How to Create the Nimble Organization* (John Wiley & Sons, 1998).[1]

Another organizational change model that follows a similar philosophy to the Burning Platform is John Kotter's eight-step model of organizational change.

John Kotter's Eight-Step Model of Organizational Change

Dr. John Kotter, the Harvard professor regarded by many as the authority on leadership and change, has written another book for this method of change. His easy-to-read business parable, *Our Iceberg Is Melting* (Macmillan, 2006), uses a short, insightful parable of a penguin who learns of impending disaster that will affect the entire colony. The ice flow the colony lives on is about to break up. This one little penguin is faced with convincing the leaders of the colony to move thousands of birds immediately. Dr. Kotter's writings aren't limited to a cute parable. Two of his other books are *A Sense of Urgency* (Harvard Business Review Press, 2008) and *The Heart of Change: Real-Life Stories of How People Change Their Organizations* (Harvard Business Review Press, 2012).

Kotter has developed an eight-step model for using the Melting Iceberg metaphor to change an organization[2]:

1. Establish a sense of urgency.
   Leaders must be infected with this same sense of urgency and be able to instill it in their people.

2. Create a guiding coalition.
   A team of leaders must align together to solve the problem. Division of power will cause delay, and lack of focus will cause failure.

3. Develop a change vision.

You must develop a clear vision that is easily understood, believed, and doable.

4. Communicate the vision and gain buy-in.

Learn who the influencers and change agents are in your organization. Get them on board and help them spread the word.

5. Empower people for a foundation of action.

Give people the power to make necessary change. Pressuring people to make change but not giving them the power and resources is incredibly demotivating.

6. Generate short-term wins.

Divide long-term projects into short-term winnable goals. Celebrate reaching these short-term goals to increase motivation.

7. Never let up.

Use the momentum of short-term wins to keep going.

8. Incorporate change into the culture.

Become a learning organization that looks for continual improvement.

Dr. Kotter goes into detail and includes numerous stories of organizations making change in his books *The Heart of Change* and *A Sense of Urgency*.

Whether you call it Burning Platform or Melting Iceberg, this model of people, process, and culture change has a high failure rate. That is probably due to the fact that many executives use it when the platform or colony isn't in true life-threatening danger. This method does work when the people believe their leaders, when they can see and believe the imminent threat, and when the leadership creates a clear direction and process of how the organization can be saved and even come out better.

There is a problem with this method that reflects on leadership. The sense of urgency that is needed by Kotter's Melting Iceberg and the Burning Platform, implies impending doom. This suggests that management was not aware of what was ahead. Management waited until there was impending disaster and is now depending on crisis mode to fix it.

Culture

- If the organizational culture is composed of high-energy, proactive people (think Silicon Valley start-up culture) who feel they have a stake in a winning outcome, this model can be highly successful.

- If the organizational culture is hierarchical and motivated to the cause—for example, military units and some highly structured business units—this model can be successful if the cause is true.

- If the organizational culture is more bureaucratic and less self-directed, and people have an attitude of "just follow orders," there's a greater chance of failure.

Situation

- If this isn't a do-or-die situation and your people discover they have been misled, then you lose credibility and motivation and may face internal sabotage.

- Teams and entire organizations can go through this successfully once or twice, but if this happens once a year or more, everyone will just ignore it. While working in a do-or-die environment can be exhilarating, most people will put their lives and families on hold only a few times for business. At some point they realize they don't want to stay in that organization.

Outcome

- If you are truly in a once-in-a-decade do-or-die situation and you get people aligned and motivated, this model can create amazing results—the "land a man on the moon" kind of results. However, for most day-to-day changes this model has a high failure rate.

Trapeze Theory Model of Organizational Change

For an individual in an organization, cultural change is like taking that first leap from a platform to catch a swinging trapeze. There's fear of the unknown, the gathering of energy to overcome inertia, and the uncertainty of outcome. Even with all the negatives, change does happen—the fear is balanced by the thrill of learning new skills and the potential for applause and recognition.

As executives or managers in marketing, we need to find ways to increase our people's chances of making that leap, catching a swinging trapeze, and timing the landing on a new platform. The more successfully we can help our people make this transition, the more successful we will be.

Any marketing organization that faces the New Marketing Mandate to switch into data-driven marketing will face some unease and inertia. It is just as important for you as a manager to create a plan to manage the people and process changes as it is to manage the technology changes. We feel that a combination of John Kotter's steps at the highest level and the Trapeze Theory model at the support level is the best way to help people move in three stages from their old platform through the uncertainty of change to the new platform.

Where We Are	Midair	Where We Want to Be
How do we motivate people to leave their comfort zone?	How do we make sure they fly through the transition?	How do we make sure they land safely and stay there?
Acknowledge the fear—almost everyone fears their first solo. Let them know that is normal.	Catcher (mentor)—Have someone experienced ready to catch them in midair.	Have a catcher—Have someone grab their hand when they land to help them keep their balance.
Training—Make sure they have practiced in realistic situations so they have confidence they can do it.	Stretch—Let people know they may have to stretch to meet their goals during the transition.	Applause—Make sure the applause is motivating. Some like to hear it privately, others like it loud and public.
Increase their strength—If they aren't strong enough, build them up.	Safety harness—A practice harness lets people take a risk.	Larger platform—Make the new platform easier to land on and stay on.

Where We Are	Midair	Where We Want to Be
Smaller platform—Reduce support for the old way. If the old ways take more work and are riskier than the new ways, there's less reason to stay.	Decrease the height—Reduce the danger of making a mistake.	Tell the stories—Share the positive stories so they learn from others' experiences.
Fire—Light a fire so it is uncomfortable or riskier to stay on the old platform.	Applause—Make sure they can hear the applause for those who have reached the other side.	Fix mistakes—When someone stumbles, adapt the training or fix the system so it doesn't happen again.
Recognition—Some people like constant change, others like occasional change, and still others like no change. Can you find a place for multiple types?	Net—Don't let a mistake be fatal. If a mistake can potentially cause serious issues, make sure a mentor oversees.	Keep practicing—Don't stop. After landing, take a breath to recover. Then, while the exhilaration is still there, do it again.
Give them a ladder down and out—Some people would rather leave than change. Make it easy and gracious for them to leave without demotivating others.	Get back on—If someone falls, help them get back up so they can do it the right way before negative memories or habits set it.	Reinforce the new platform—Make the new platform a more inviting place to be than the old.

The Trapeze Theory model works well with the Burning Platform. The Trapeze Theory model helps support people as they go through the steps necessary to move away from the Burning Platform.

In the situation of helping your marketing organization move to a higher level of maturity, you can look at the Trapeze Theory model to understand where people might have fear of the unknown, where they need more time or practice, and where they need training and instructions. Marketers may want to go back to the old platform, their old way of doing things. That's when managers need to use discipline and coaching skills to reinforce the new direction. Use the Trapeze Theory model to help executives, managers, and all marketers understand they will be going through a time of change.

COMMON BARRIERS TO INCREASING MATURITY AND HOW TO BREAK THROUGH

Whether you are proactively changing to stay ahead of the New Marketing Mandate or you are changing in incremental steps, you will face barriers that can be even more daunting than the adoption of new technology. Remember that the New Marketing Mandate needs people, process, and technology. The common barriers described next are a big picture view of barriers you will see at different stages.

There are common barriers that every organization faces as it moves between stages in the Customer Experience Maturity Model. The following sections describe the large common barriers and what you can do to go around them, over them, or under them. The following chapters dedicated to the stages in the Customer Experience Maturity Model discuss in depth the barriers you may face at each specific stage.

Barrier 1: Lack of Understanding Return on Investment (Early Stages)

It can be a huge task going from business-as-usual traditional marketing to data-driven customer experience marketing. This barrier comes from not understanding the value that comes when data-driven marketing improves customer experience. Many marketers seem to think this type of marketing is appropriate only for e-commerce marketing; however, no matter what your line of business and industry is, all marketing organizations can use the steps of the Customer Experience Maturity Model to improve their customers' experience.

If this is a barrier for you, consider using some of the cases from this book to create your business case. Also consider starting your change with the quick wins (described in Chapter 8, Stage 4— Optimize, and Chapter 13, Selling to the Board), to prove the effects of making these changes.

Barrier 2: Lack of Strategic Direction (Early Stages)

Ask yourself and your team, "Why does our website exist?" If you get answers like "Branding," "To be better than our competitors," or "To inform customers about our company and services," you are facing a lack of strategic direction.

What you should be getting are answers that support your organization's strategic objectives, which in many cases are objectives such as increase revenue, reduce costs, and increase customer loyalty. You must also pay attention to what metrics you use to report digital marketing success. If the metrics are ones such as visits, page views, time on site, and likes, then you are not strategic. To break through this barrier, you need to align strategic objectives with marketing objectives and digital goals so it is clear to everyone how digital is an important driver in the business.

Barrier 3: Lack of Resources, or How to Focus the Resources You Have (Early to Middle Stages)

Today's marketer and marketing teams have a lot on their plates, from branding to producing content, from events to launch campaigns, from looking at data to reports. So adding new tasks may be too much and overwhelming, as there simply isn't time for doing more.

A sign that your teams are overwhelmed is when they say they can't do testing and personalization because doing so requires more content, content they don't have time to produce.

If you are facing this barrier, consider starting at a point where you can create an impact with a small amount of content, and use that to prove your case for additional resources. If that is not possible, consider starting a small guerrilla project where you use external consultants to help.

Barrier 4: Caught in a Technology Silo (Middle Stages)

Some organizations are mature in their use of technology; many larger organizations typically use web content management, web analytics, marketing automation, testing, social integration, and the like. They can be quite sophisticated in their use and have built internal experts who know how to use these tools to produce value.

Typically, we see these organizations failing to move past the Nurture stage, because all the tools they use are different tools. The inability to integrate the tools presents an insurmountable barrier.

Web content management needs to be integrated with web analytics for tracking digital goal conversions within a site, but it also needs to be:

- Integrated with marketing automation, so triggers and behavior can be read from the sites

- Integrated with a testing tool, so you don't have to copy and paste content between the systems

- Integrated with social channels, so it's easy to provide reports and analysis on social channels that work with other digital channels

If you consider web analytics that need integration with testing and segmentation, they also need to be:

- Integrated with marketing automation, to track effectiveness of campaigns and compare those to other initiatives captured by the web analytics tool

- Integrated with social, so you can add demographics data to where you have analytics and track the effect of using social channels

And all of these integration barriers and issues continue with each additional technology that is part of digital marketing. If the technology isn't integrated, it becomes difficult and expensive to overcome the barriers at higher stages in the Customer Experience Maturity Model. Perhaps the most serious failing with nonintegrated platforms is the danger of losing customers as you attempt to move through these technical barriers. The key to avoiding these types of barriers is to adopt a connected platform early in your growth up the Customer Experience Maturity Model.

Barrier 5: Lack of Executive Buy-In (Middle Stages)

Once you enter Stage 6, customer insights from different systems like customer relationship management (CRM), customer service, loyalty management, and finance are needed to create the single view of the customer. Creating the single view of the customer across online and offline touch points involves many different teams in your organization that cross many functions.

One of the biggest barriers is not having executive buy-in. In fact, many studies have shown that one of the chief reasons for large project failure is the lack of executive buy-in. Without executive buy-in it's very difficult for one team to initiate cross-organizational projects and get full commitment from other organizational teams.

We strongly advocate the emerging executive role of the chief digital officer (CDO) or chief marketing technologist (CMT), who has the skills to combine strategy, technology, and marketing and has the mandate to make sure that cross-organizational projects are aligned to create the single view of the customer.

To see how the barriers you face compare to the barriers in other similar organizations, go to the book's companion website, www.ConnectTheExperience.com/barriers.

NOTES

1. Daryl Conner, "The Real Story of the Burning Platform," August 15, 2012, www.connerpartners.com/frameworks-and-processes/the-real-story-of-the -burning-platform.
2. Dr. John Kotter, "The 8-Step Process for Leading Change," www.kotter international.com/our-principles/changesteps.

CHAPTER 6

Stage 1—Initiate, and Stage 2—Radiate

Don't treat your customers like a bunch of purses and wallets.

—Chris Brogan

In the Initiate stage, organizations use a "brochure site" presence on the web with email campaign capabilities and web analytics (see Figure 6.1).

In the Radiate stage, organizations focus on distributing content across channels starting with the customer's most used channels. Examples include establishing a mobile site and sharing content on social networks (see Figure 6.1).

THE INITIATE AND RADIATE STAGES

The Initiate stage is almost a rite of passage for any organization. As you learned in Chapter 4, 85.4 percent of organizations surveyed with the Customer Experience Maturity Assessment are still in Stage 1 or Stage 2. The vast majority are here because they aren't sure how to progress and they have trouble building a business case for the resources to improve.

The initial website in Stage 1, Initiate, is almost always oriented around the organization's products and services rather than having a customer-centric or problem/solution orientation. That happens because the website is usually created by a marketing department or agency that has little experience with the digital customer experience

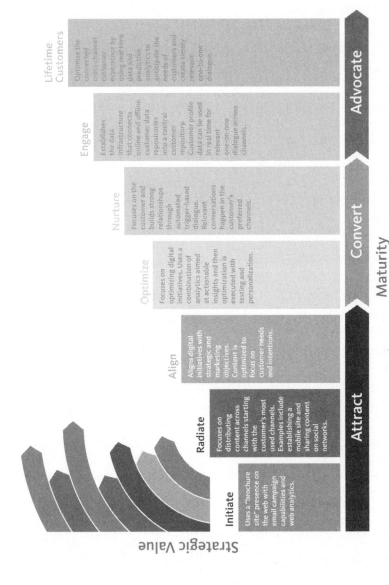

Figure 6.1 Sitecore® Customer Experience Maturity Model™—Initiate and Radiate Stages

so they pour printed marketing material into a new online format. The first attempt at connecting with customers is usually an email newsletter with a wide range of topics that is broadcast to all website registrants. The broadcast is usually informational and doesn't have specific calls to action.

At this stage, even in some midsize organizations, web analytics are limited to the volume of visitors and the number of conversions. There is no A/B testing or content evaluation, so content strategy and landing page optimization are often left to opinion. The lack of testing combined with a lack of content strategy around customer segments and stages usually result in random acts of marketing that include a lot of wasted effort.

At some point the organization becomes aware that it needs to reach out and meet its customers. An oft-heard cry is: "We need a social media presence" or "We need mobile." At this point there may still be no content strategy, analytics, or segment targeting.

In Stage 2, Radiate, marketing organizations are more concerned with reaching their customers through the appropriate channels. They begin to develop strategies for each channel, but they may not have effective ways to measure cross-channel performance. Analytics still focuses on the number of visitors and conversions, but the data is segmented by channel.

Content begins to change in Stage 2 as it becomes more relevant to the customer through channels and devices such as mobile and social. With marketing's increased awareness of the possibilities, the marketers begin to create campaigns tailored to specific segments by channel, device, and customer segment. The marketing organization tries to leverage word of mouth through social channels to spread its message.

Objectives of Initiate and Radiate

The main objectives of Initiate stage are:

- Creating a web presence with general information about the organization.

- Focusing on search engine optimization to drive more visitors.

- Communicating to customers using email.

The main objectives of Radiate stage are:

- Widening the organization's digital presence across multiple channels.

- Reaching customers through mobile and social channels with context-appropriate content.

- Increasing the organization's marketing presence across paid, owned, and earned media.

CASE STORY: CHESTER ZOO

Chester Zoo, in the United Kingdom, has the customer at the heart of its mobile strategy, focusing on the connected experience during visits to the zoo.

Together with its digital agency, the zoo's managers found that using mobile could enhance the experience for their customers. They focused on reducing time in queues and giving directions in the zoo.

Their mobile experience effectively reuses content that is also used on their website and enhances it using the native features in the mobile phone. Visitors now have a better experience because they can skip the queues by purchasing their admission tickets through a mobile shop created by the zoo's own development team. In return, visitor flow into the zoo has improved significantly during peak hours. While in the zoo, visitors can use their mobile devices to get advice on what to see and activities during the day.

Simon Hacking, online marketing manager at Chester Zoo, said: "Providing an excellent experience for visitors to our website before, during, and after their visit is very important to us and that makes mobile a crucial aspect of our strategy. Using our experience platform as a foundation for this approach means that we can publish our content once and have it instantly available to our visitors on desktop, tablet, mobile, and our iPhone and Android apps."

The results of this strategy, focusing on the customer experience, was breathtaking. Mobile phone traffic has increased by 37 percent, conversion rate has increased by 105 percent, transactions have increased by 181 percent, and revenue coming from mobile has increased by 129 percent.

If they had not had a strategy that focused on the mobile customer they would have missed big opportunities.

The next step for Chester Zoo is enabling additional mobile capability as part of the zoo experience.

MARKETING IS UNDER ATTACK ON TWO FRONTS

It used to be so easy to be a marketer, but that's no longer true! Now marketers face a revolution on two fronts—the very fronts that should be marketing allies. One battlefront is the consumers, the audience a marketer wants to learn from, engage with, and influence. On the other battlefront are the executives in the marketer's own organization. Multiple research reports show that 50 percent to 80 percent of executives don't trust their own marketers. This chapter shows you how marketing can ally itself with its audience. Chapter 7, Stage 3—Align, shows you how marketers can align with executives and business objectives.

As mentioned at the beginning of the book, the days of only a few channels has passed. There are more than 40 online and offline channels, and each channel is full of marketing messages.[1] People are overwhelmed with marketing messages.

In all of this, people have taken control of their own buyer's journey. They can choose which channels they travel on in their journey, they can choose the time that's best for them, and they can search for the specific information they need. Whether your organization is B2B, B2C, government, or nonprofit, it doesn't matter. Your customers are in control. Marketers no longer control the gates to information. As the research by CEB stated in Chapter 1, B2B buyers are 57 percent of their way through the purchase decision before engaging with sales.[2]

In the past, most websites and digital marketing were built with two motivations. Content was written from the organization's view of its products, and writing was slanted to rank high in search engines. Context was rarely considered.

Although these two motivators make it easy for an organization to create content, content alone typically fails to satisfy or influence the buyer. Content architecture is oriented to match the organization's structure, not the buyer's needs. Product or service terms are technical rather than solution-oriented. All buyers are considered to be at the same stage in the decision journey, and the channels that messages go through are the ones the organization is comfortable with, not the channels the buyer prefers. With all that, it's amazing that buyers put up with it.

In fact, informed buyers don't put up with it. What informed buyers do is either stick with what they have or switch to an organization that connects and engages with them.

To engage and be relevant to our customers, we as marketers must engage them in both content and context. The content must be relevant to their specific needs and at the correct point in the buyer's journey. The context must be relevant to their physical location and the type of device they use. If your content and context aren't relevant to your audience, you will lose them to a competitor who can do that.

Most marketers are aware that content must match the visitor segment and the visitor's stage in the Customer Life Cycle. However, not all marketers have thought about the more recent addition of "context." Context is the "how and where" of the marketing message.

Organizations in Stage 1, Initiate, have websites that show static content and are perhaps using a mass email newsletter to an undifferentiated audience. These marketers use static content with formatting designed for standard desktop screens. Their email newsletter is primarily organization-centric, sending the same message to all audiences with information that is more important to the organization than to the individual needs of customers. In effect, marketers published with a take-it or leave-it attitude. In this chapter we see how to make sure that the content in even a Stage 1 website fits the needs of the audience.

This chapter also helps you move to Stage 2, Radiate. In Radiate marketers adapt to the "how and where" of the visitor's context. If the marketers want their message to "radiate" outward they must use the channels customers prefer, create content that adapts to the visitor's buying situation and physical location, and content that adapts to the technical capabilities of the customer's device. These requirements make moving up to Stage 2, Radiate, sound like a complex task, but the processes in this chapter show you how to keep it in control.

As you think about moving into Stage 2, Radiate, it may be easiest to consider the four primary ways of radiating to customers. Remember that not all of these ways are worth doing for all organizations. The four primary ways of radiating to consider are,

1. Web

    • Responsive web design that adapts to small screens in portrait or landscape orientation

    • Touch responsive screens rather than keyboard and mouse

    • Optimized images that adapt to small screens and lower bandwidth

    • Concise content that doesn't have a high word count

2. Email

    • Email lists segmented and contextualized to the needs of visitor segments

    • Responsive email design that adapts to the visitor's device

3. Social media

    • Messaging that fits the social community it targets

    • Messaging that fits within small screen and message limits

    • Social marketing programs that use the social network to spread the organization's message

4. Apps and device capabilities

    • Downloadable apps that take advantage of capabilities built-in to mobile devices such as coupons that appear when GeoIP detects you are near a store.

How you choose to radiate out and the priorities you set depend on your business model and customer needs. In general, email has the highest impact. For most organizations one of the most impactful first steps they can take in radiating is to find the needs of their customers and begin with consistent email focused on solving the problems of specific customer segments. This does not take a heavy time and resource involvement and can lead into more automated programs, as described in Chapter 9, Stage 5, Nurture. However, when you create your marketing and customer experience plan consider the cost of buying a system that has email segmentation and automation built-in compared to the cost of having to convert data and possibly lose subscribers if you move from a basic system to a connected one you will need next year.

After establishing email campaign capabilities most organizations add basic social capabilities using LinkedIn, Facebook, Twitter, Pinterest, or one of the other myriad of social networks that are most used by customers. The social marketing is needed to support your brand and to monitor your customer's thoughts and opinions.

The high growth of smartphone usage has created equivalent high growth in mobile Internet use and smartphone apps. What we see in our consulting with organizations worldwide is organizations moving up from their Stage 1 or Stage 2 "one size fits all" designs to designs that are mobile responsive so they can take immediate advantage of the growth in mobile internet access.

Benefits to Your Customer

The term *customer-centric marketing* should be a redundancy, but too often we see websites and digital marketing that are not customer-centric. Instead the website is oriented around the organization's products and delivery, and the digital marketing outreach is oriented to meet the organization's marketing silos. This should be sacrilege to marketers who care about their customers and about meeting objectives.

Using the processes described later in this chapter, you will be able to create experiences that are customer-centric. Your customers will benefit in multiple ways. Following the processes described in this chapter will ensure that your customers find content with topics that fit their personas or their customer segments and the stage they are at in their decision journey. Customers will move faster through the decision journey if they not only have the right content at the right time and in the preferred channel, but also if you have used calls to action and psychological triggers that help them identify their needs and make a decision.

When customers find what they are looking for and the message is relevant to their needs and stage, then they are much more likely to trust the message. It makes them aware that you understand them.

With customers using so many digital channels, it is important that you connect with your customers through the context that is most relevant to them. You want to connect through the right device, at the right time, and in the right format. Marketing messages should be in the primary channel used by a customer segment or persona.

You can see that a development strategy for Stage 2, Radiate, is not just about sending messages out through multiple channels. Rather, a more integrated strategy is to use all the channels together to build trust and commitment with your audience. With a family entertainment park, for example, managers can use their website to attract visitors and build interest. They can then use email to nurture visitors and inform them of coming events related to their interests. Social channels can be used to give testimonials and endorsements for how good it is and to show pictures of people having fun. And finally, when a visitor arrives smartphone users can find current events, performance information, and reserve tickets. It all works together to create a better customer experience.

Benefits to Your Organization

Organizations that use the processes described in this chapter benefit in two primary ways. They know what to focus their limited resources on, and they build marketing processes with more conversions, faster velocity, and higher advocacy.

Almost every marketing organization we've spoken with in the past three years has complained about its limited resources. When you have limited resources, you have to focus your work on those areas where you get the greatest leverage and impact. Following the process in this chapter helps you do that. We have found that Pareto's rule, 80/20, applies here as well. About 20 percent of the content and 20 percent of your marketing produce 80 percent of the results. This process identifies the 20 percent you need to focus on.

When you present your customers with the content they need at the time they need it and you prep their minds with a psychological trigger so they are ready for a specific call to action, then you have created great marketing. Your marketing is more engaging and more relevant.

So what happens to organizations that engage their customers and that become obsessed with being relevant? Research shows that engaged customers become advocates. As advocates, customers trust your organization and commit to a longer relationship. They gain by making better purchases because they trust the information about your products and services. They don't waste time or expense. It becomes a virtuous cycle that benefits both customer and organization.

As an organization, you win when your customers become advocates. Research shows that advocates are two to three times more effective than nonadvocates in persuading others to purchase.[3] Other research shows that advocates give you immediate payback by spending twice as much as the average customer as well as sharing their recommendations two to four times more than an average customer.[4]

PROCESS FOR IDENTIFYING CRITICAL CONTENT

The process described below is an excellent process to follow if you are developing a new site. For a new site the process will keep you focused on what is critical to success and help you use your limited resources wisely. If you have an existing site and are either moving it to a new technology or improving it using the same technology, the work you do in the following process will give you and your customers all the benefits described in the previous section.

The process described here builds the foundation for all customer-centric sites and digital marketing. This foundation requires:

- Customer segmentation or personas

- Decision journey

- Digital Relevancy Map (DRM)

- Content audit

If you aren't sure your marketing organization has a customer-centric orientation, you can be sure that working through this process will change marketing's frame of reference. In the following process you will:

- Identify your most important types of customers using either visitor segmentation or personas.

- Map your customer's journey discovering key junctions and decision points.

- Identify the content, needs, customer intent, and call to action for each customer and stage in the customer's journey.

- Identify the channel that is best for each customer and stage.

Identifying Your Customers and Visitors

You can't sell to everyone. That's a basic truism that every salesperson and marketer should know in his or her heart.

Most organizations have three or four principal types of people who are their target customers. Understanding these types is essential to connecting and engaging with them. You must know what are their needs and drivers, their psychological triggers, their intent at each stage in marketing, and how you can identify them. Two ways of identifying your customers are personas and customer segmentation.

You will be using customer segments (or personas, which are different) to identify the unique intent and need of each, the types of content that generate the most engagement, the types of messaging that build trust, and the paths each segment (or persona) takes.

Personas

Personas are miniature personality sketches that help marketers understand and know their customer types. Many large marketing organizations have already created personas to help marketers understand to whom they are marketing.

Personas are meant to convey real awareness of customers' behavior, not just explicit details that help identify them. Personas often include photos and describe personal attributes about their lifestyles, needs, and aspirations.

Personas and the behaviors they imply are very important to personalization in marketing. For more in-depth descriptions about mapping personas to content, see Chapter 8, Stage 4—Optimize.

Two very simple personas for the purpose of this chapter could be:

Eric

Eric is a "Family Adventurer." He likes to travel with his wife Kathy and their two small children to exciting and educational locations. They are always looking for "good deals" in their travels and will wait for the right price. Both of them are full-time teachers. That means they have a large block of time available during school vacations.

Eric often searches the web together with Kathy for good travel deals using a few bookmarked websites and a lot of online searching. Many of the "good deals" they buy are through a few referral sites, which can be identified. They are especially interested in European travel to historic locations that are part of "family saver packages."

Dean

Dean is the "Backpacker Traveler." He is budget conscious, but young and adventurous, and could have a little risk taker in him. He is willing to stay in a wide range of accommodations ranging from tent camping, to hostels, to entry-level hotels. Although he carries everything in his backpack, he likes to get to an area and then stay for a few weeks as he explores all the local adventures.

Dean finds his next adventure by searching travel forums and looking through online adventure magazines. He works a lot by word of mouth, and it is difficult to market to him through normal marketing channels. However, once he trusts you as a source you're golden.

Customer Segmentation

Visitor segmentation groups potential prospects who have similar characteristics. These characteristics are identified more by explicit data.

(Personas may use behavioral data for identification.) Customer segmentation is often done with explicit identifiers that can be found using traditional web analytics. For some web content management systems it is easy to create personalized content or marketing based on these explicit identifiers.

Some examples of explicit identifiers that could be used to segment customers are:

GeoIP	Keywords	Internal search keywords
Traffic source	Referrer source	Campaigns
Landing page	Visit number	New visitor
Registration details		

Examples of visitor segments that use explicit identifiers are:

Persona or Segment	Brief Description	Explicit Data
Newbie	New visitor	First visit
		PPC landing page
		Search engine
Returning visitor	Has visited the site at least one time in the past 30 days	Days since first visit
		PPC landing page
		Search engine
Interested visitor	Registered and downloaded special offer from campaign	Registration details
		Deep page views
		Email landing page
Purchaser	Has made a purchase on the site	Registration details
		Landing page
		Completed purchase

To Do: Create Visitor Segments

Identify the characteristics of your three or four primary customer segments and write them in the following table. If you already have personas created, use them but complete the additional columns.

This information will be essential for completing the Digital Relevancy Map, which is the culmination of this chapter. The companion website to this book has templates of many tables from the book. Please refer to www.ConnectTheExperience.com/templates.

Segment Name	Character-istics	Identifiers	Primary Channel	Customer Intent	Content Example
Newbie (Example)	New to our experience No knowledge May need help and a special offer to register	New visitor Days since first visit PPC landing page	Search engine	Learn basics about what we have to offer compared to competitors	Home page experience that drives guest to learn pages
Visitor Segment 2					
Visitor Segment 3					
Visitor Segment 4					

Planning Your Customer's Journey

All customers take paths through the experiences you provide. The customer journey may involve wandering through your website, absorbing newsletter content, participating in a social media event, or many other paths. This wandering creates a customer journey that if done correctly ends with you achieving your marketing objective and the customer engaging with you as a lifetime customer. It's important to understand each stage of this journey, so you can evaluate whether you have the right channel, right message, and right content for each stage. If you are missing one of these touch points or it is wrong, then it is time to create new marketing and new content to assist your customer in making a favorable decision.

Most customer journeys look something like Figure 6.2.

Importantly, the customer journey map highlights what we need to deliver to meet visitors' needs or to shorten, accelerate, or reinforce their journey. There may be different journeys for each of your

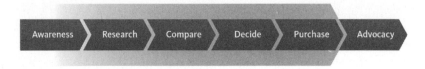

Figure 6.2   Customer Journey Map

important visitor segments. Some segments may enter at a different point on the journey; for example, a business analyst might enter at the beginning to do research, whereas a manager might enter at the decision stage after having read a report from the analyst.

The customer journey map can also show us the failure points, the places where marketing fails. While marketers might like to think of visitors moving through a marketing funnel from first contact to becoming a qualified lead, few marketing funnels move the visitor on a straight path. Many paths involve longer-term involvement with repeating cycles of nurture, test, modify, and repeat. Each time through this cycle, the visitor is given the opportunity and motivation to move closer to completing the commitment. This repeating cycle enables customers to enter with a low level of risk and engagement and take baby steps, gradually increasing their engagement and commitment at a comfortable rate.

These nurture/test/reward cycles should be built so that visitors are nurtured to a point where the marketer can give them a test of commitment—for example, a discount coupon in exchange for a registration with a detailed personal profile. If the visitors complete that profile, they pass the test and get their reward of a discount coupon. If they don't complete the profile, they fall back into the previous nurture path. This gradually increasing cycle builds with more commitment needed and greater rewards until the visitor is fully committed.

To Do: Map Your Customer Journey

Work with your marketing team to identify the typical journey for your customers. A good way to do this is to gather six or eight experienced channel marketers, marketing strategists, salespeople, and customer services people in a conference room with stacks of large Post-it Notes. Use the Post-it Notes to brainstorm and rearrange customer journey maps until you come to one that works for your major visitor segments.

Do not make a customer journey that is too complex. You will be creating content for each stage in the journey and each visitor segment. If you have four visitor segments and five stages in the journey, then there will be 20 distinct content-context cells. It quickly multiplies into an overwhelming amount of work. So make it real, but keep it simple.

What stages in the customer journey do your marketers use to envision customer or visitor movement? This is a sample of one possible customer journey.

Stage	Description
Awareness	Customer becomes aware of us, considers working with us, and wants to learn more.
Research	Customer is researching and comparing products, narrowing down the choices.
Compare	Customer is planning the purchase and selecting options.
Decide	Customer makes the decision to commit.
Purchase	Customer commits and returns to website to manage the delivery and ongoing engagements.

Some other customer journeys might look like the following:

Research > Decide > Convert

Needs > Search > Evaluate > Decision > Engage > Support

Awareness > Acquisition > Evaluation > Decision > Conversion > Advocacy

By mapping the customer's start point, intentions at each stage, and end point, we can better understand the customer journey through the site and marketing touch points. Once we know these paths, we can shape the customer's path through the site and ensure that the most relevant content and the most powerful calls to action are more visible. You will have a chance to do this at the end of this chapter in the Digital Relevancy Map.

It's Not Just Content; It's Also Context

In decades past, marketers controlled the context of their message. They knew with 80 percent certainty that their prospective customers would be watching a specific television show or standing at a bus stop and reading a billboard. Often it wasn't just the location context that was assumed. Often marketers assumed everyone was at the top of the funnel, so everyone was served content written for the top of the funnel. It was up to the sales force to bring customers through the rest of the sales journey. Those days are in the past.

Context also implies location and stage in the customer journey. Twenty-seven percent of customers use a mobile device when researching a product or service online.[5] Estimates are that by 2015 there will be more people using mobile than desktop Internet access.[6]

Even with that type of pressure for mobile marketing, most organizations have still not adapted as well as you might think. Our research, outlined in Chapter 4, shows that 52 percent of websites still need to be optimized for mobile users. It is next to impossible for customers in any industry to have a good experience if they are looking at a desktop website through a handheld mobile device.

The mobile context also changes how content is served. Mobile devices have many screen resolutions and capabilities. Putting your content into the wrong format or using videos that are inaccessible could lose many of your customers.

Another context you must be aware of is the customer's context within the decision journey. A customer just entering the journey has completely different needs and intent than a customer ready to make a final commitment. If you serve the wrong content at the wrong stage in the customer journey, you could lose or slow down a customer.

Examples of reaching out to customers to give them the experience and solutions they need abound in both small and large companies. Some of our large B2B customers are using mobile sites so their customers' field engineers can go to the mobile site, look for a solution that fits very specific engineering requirements, and order it online. A more local example is the successful owner of a lawn care business checked a photo sent to his iPhone by one of his crew 40 miles away. The owner then researched the hard-to-find irrigation part on his iPhone, called the supplier, and had the part waiting for his repair crew to pick up. He was beating his competitors with great quality work and timely service, all made possible by adapting to a customer-centric mobile experience. The world is changing for every type of organization. You must adapt.

Creating the Digital Relevancy Map

The Sitecore Digital Relevancy Map (DRM) is a framework that shows the content appropriate for each of your major visitors' segments at each stage in their customer journey. The DRM is useful for all organizations. It is a way to optimize the experience for your customers.

We created the Digital Relevancy Map as a framework for mapping the intent and context of customers as they move through the different stages of their decision journey. The DRM has been invaluable in our consulting.

A few of the advantages of mapping your content with a DRM are that it:

- Focuses marketing's work on the 20 percent of content that does 80 percent of the work.

- Focuses content developers on the customer's intent, need, and call to action for each piece of content.

- Reduces "random acts of content."

- Identifies missing pieces of information.

- Accelerates customers through their journey.

- Helps identify where and what to test when there are leaks in the customer journey.

The DRM is a large table. Down the left side of the table are names for each of your visitor segments or personas. Across the top of the table are the stages of the customer journey. This produces a matrix of cells, with one cell for each visitor segment and stage in the customer journey.

Your DRM will be unique to your organization. It should use your visitor segments and the stages in your customer journey. Once it is filled in it will contain descriptions that are very specific to your website and marketing.

Using Analytics to Assist in Building the DRM

Traditional web analytics can be used to discover and validate explicit metrics and criteria that define customer segments. In most cases an experienced analyst will already have a good idea which criteria will produce customer segments with good results.

If you are already using Experience Analytics, as defined in Chapter 7, Stage 3—Align, and you have identified high-interest visitor segments or personas, then creating the DRM will be easier.

To Do: Create Your Digital Relevancy Map

After you complete the earlier exercises in this chapter, create the following table using your visitor segments down the left side and the stages in your customer journey across the top. The companion website to this book has templates of many tables from the book. Please refer to www.ConnectTheExperience.com/templates.

	Acquire	Research	Purchase	Advocate
Visitor Segment 1	Intent: Attract attention. Pique interest.	Intent: Browsing solutions. Will I use it? Is it cool?	Intent: Is this the best choice? Compare alternatives.	Intent: Spread the word how great it is! (How cool you are!)
	How Can Intent Be Revealed?: Nonbranded keywords, PPC general ads, browsing pages on site	How Can Intent Be Revealed?: Branded keywords, PPC deep ads, focus on specific pages, response to email	How Can Intent Be Revealed?: Direct URL, feature and comparison tables, pricing, store locator	How Can Intent Be Revealed?: Social sharing, forward offers
	Touch Points: Search, PPC	Touch Points: Search, PPC, email, social	Touch Points: Email nurture, social, nurture, custom direct mail	Touch Points: Social, email share
	Their Objective: Discovery	Their Objective: Narrow alternatives	Their Objective: Am I sure?	Their Objective: Help friends, gain status

	Acquire	Research	Purchase	Advocate
	Our Objective: Create awareness and interest	Our Objective: Imagine themselves in the experience, create desire, unique selling proposition	Our Objective: Reduce friction	Our Objective: Spread the word. You can do it!
	Persuasive Content Needed: Increase interest, high-energy adventure videos that trigger experiences, accessible info, everyone can do it	Persuasive Content Needed: Experience video, average guy shots, image shots, event tie-ins	Persuasive Content Needed: Testimonials, "Never thought I would, but I love it!," images of product with major players	Persuasive Content Needed: Share the experience. Join the fun!
Visitor Segment 2	Intent:	Intent:	Intent:	Intent:
	How Can Intent Be Revealed?:	How Can Intent Be Revealed?:	How Can Intent Be Revealed?:	How Can Intent Be Revealed?:
	Touch Points:	Touch Points:	Touch Points:	Touch Points:
	Their Objective:	Their Objective:	Their Objective:	Their Objective:
	Our Objective:	Our Objective:	Our Objective:	Our Objective:
	Persuasive Content Needed:	Persuasive Content Needed:	Persuasive Content Needed:	Persuasive Content Needed:

Here are tips on the items in each cell.

Intent. What is the customer's intent at this point? What do we need to do to help customers reach their goals? Take each customer segment and outline the path they should take through information and goals. The aim is to reinforce the customers' intent with decisions that move them to the next stage in the customer journey. Some examples of intent are:

- Does it fit my price/need?
- Is this the best choice?
- Do I qualify?
- How does this compare?

How Can Intent Be Revealed? What can be used to identify the customer's intent? Are there explicit or implicit behaviors that will reveal the user's intent? Some examples of how the intention can be revealed are:

- Keywords
- Topics or product sections in the site
- Use of an online calculator
- Pages selected
- Campaign entered with

Touch Points. What are the different touch points where the customer is touched by marketing? Can the customer connection be personalized at these touch points?

- Website
- Mobile
- Email
- Point of sale

Their Objective. What do customers want to accomplish at the website? What are they looking for?

- Check out of the shopping cart.
- Find a specific product.

- Find ratings.

- Compare to a competitor.

Our Objectives. What do we want customers to do? Where do we want them to move to in their decision journey?

- Compare our product with a competitor and select our product.

- Register for product offers.

- Complete the shopping cart transaction.

- Refer a friend to the site through social connections.

Persuasive Content Needed. What is the information, download asset, video, or page that the customer needs at this point? What is appropriate content for each customer segment? This content can also be used to help identify content used in personalization for this customer segment at this stage. Some examples of content are:

- White papers or articles

- Webinars

- Testimonials or quotes

- Calculators

- Product information pages

Identifying Content to Match the DRM

Once you have completed your Digital Relevancy Map, you need to identify the content that goes into each cell. This is a fun exercise for new websites.

If you have an existing site, the audit of content and positioning of each page or asset in the DRM can work. But here's a tip. The DRM is used to help you identify the content that is most important to your customers and their journey. You can use that concept in reverse to fill in the DRM.

If you have Experience Analytics as described in Chapter 7, Stage 3—Align, then create reports showing the pages and assets that produce the highest value. If you can segment by your customer segments, then do so. Use these high-value lists to identify the content for each cell in your DRM.

If you have not yet created an Engagement Value Scale, as described in Chapter 7, use traditional analytics to identify the pages that have the highest visits or the pages and assets related to the most conversions. If you can segment by customer segments, then do so. Use these high-visit/high-conversion lists to identify the content for your DRM.

There are other ways in which the DRM can help you tailor content to your customers. A good example is the mobile experience. Depending on your type of business, a high percentage of your mobile users are using your content differently from desktop users. Chester Zoo is an excellent example of a customer experience that depends on the context. Customers planning their trips use the desktop website to research and buy travel arrangements and tickets. However, once they are close to Chester Zoo, they are using mobile. While in the mobile context they are looking for schedules and locations that are in the immediate vicinity. The content and context are completely different. How would your customer like to use your products, services, and knowledge if they could access them while they were mobile?

Before you start building your mobile site, begin with a Digital Relevancy Map. The intent, content, and call to action will almost assuredly be different, and that can change your complete mobile site design.

BREAKING BARRIERS

Having done the DRM process, we can tell you that it has elements that are a lot of fun and parts that are a hard slog. The identification of visitor segments and team discussions around intent produces a lot of insightful discussion and deeper understanding. The opposite side is that auditing the content of an existing website to determine the content you have and how it fits in the DRM can be a difficult job. Given how helpful the DRM is once complete, it is a job worth doing well.

Moving to a Higher Level of Marketing

The creation of a DRM will move your marketing team to a higher level of customer-centric marketing. One of the most important things the DRM will help you with is focusing. If you are consistent about checking the DRM before creating or posting new content, you will stop the dreaded "Random Acts of Marketing." The DRM also helps you with gap analysis, showing you content that is missing for a specific customer segment at a specific stage in their Customer Life Cycle.

Random Acts of Marketing Content!

Completing the DRM table can be done by an experienced team of channel managers in one or two meetings. We would also recommend letting it sit for a few days and then reviewing it with a fresh mind before beginning to use it to audit content.

Auditing the content on your site is much easier if you have the assistance of one or two content developers or content managers who know all the content and structure of the site. With the help of one or two content developers you can probably audit the DRM content and identify important content in the DRM in one or two concentrated days of work. However, if you have a site that has been overtaken by random acts of marketing content and you have no content developers to guide you through the site, an audit could take a week or more.

Knowing You Have Arrived

Once you have completed the DRM, it will be easier to identify where content is missing and where you need to add new content. The DRM is truly a map for how to get your visitors to your most important conversions.

Part of your internal work flow should be to add to the DRM and new content and assets. There will always be some content, such as Help and About Us, that is not part of the DRM, but that must remain as part of the infrastructure. If you can't identify where on the DRM new content should go, then you should question whether it is important.

You can use the DRM as a map for tracking loss rate and acceleration of visitors through the visitor journey. To do that, have your digital analyst segment data by visitor segments. Then the analyst should track the number of visitors and conversions at each stage. In this case a stage might consist of a specific goal conversion, or goals combined with number of visits, and so on. By comparing the rate of change between stages, you can see where visitors are accelerating, where they are slowing down, and where they are leaking.

At the Radiate stage you may make significant improvements with the addition of a mobile website and content that is tailored to mobile users and context. Moving into social channels may reveal new visitor segments and new channels for marketing. You should monitor the existing conversations and groups in social channels and learn how you can create connections to these groups. Watch for changes in attitude and sentiment through social channels, as these channels will give you more immediate feedback on your customers' feelings.

NOTES

1. David Sealey, "The BIG List of Today's Marketing Channels," May 13, 2013, www.smartinsights.com/online-brand-strategy/multichannel-strategies/selectmarketing-channels/.
2. "The Digital Evolution in B2B Marketing," CEB Marketing Leadership Council, 2012.
3. ComScore and Yahoo!, "Word of Mouth and Brand Advocate Stats," December 2006, www.zuberance.com/resources/resourcesStats.php.
4. Deloitte, "Word of Mouth and Brand Advocate Stats," March 2010, www.zuberance.com/resources/resourcesStats.php.
5. "Is Mobile Internet Taking Over Desktop Usage?," June 4, 2013, http://visual.ly/mobile-internet-taking-over-desktop-usage.
6. "The Mobile Internet Report," Morgan Stanley Research, 2010.

CHAPTER 7

Stage 3—Align

If you don't know where you're going, you'll end up somewhere else.

—Yogi Berra

Organizations in this stage align digital initiatives with strategic and marketing objectives. Content is optimized to focus on customer needs and intentions (see Figure 7.1).

THE ALIGN STAGE

The previous chapter described the revolution that's taking place in the world of business. Marketers face this revolution on two fronts, their customers and their own executives. Earlier chapters described how customers are taking control of their own buyer's journey and decision process. This chapter shows you as a marketer how you can align your marketing organization around achieving business objectives. Prove how marketing achieves strategic objectives, and you'll have the executive team on your side.

The purpose of the first part of this chapter is to show you a process you can use to align your digital goals with marketing objectives that drive strategic objectives. The second half of the chapter shows you how to get started with Experience Analytics. Experience Analytics complements traditional web analytics, but it has the advantage of showing how relevant and efficient your marketing is and also gives you one single metric to measure the value of different marketing experiences across multiple channels.

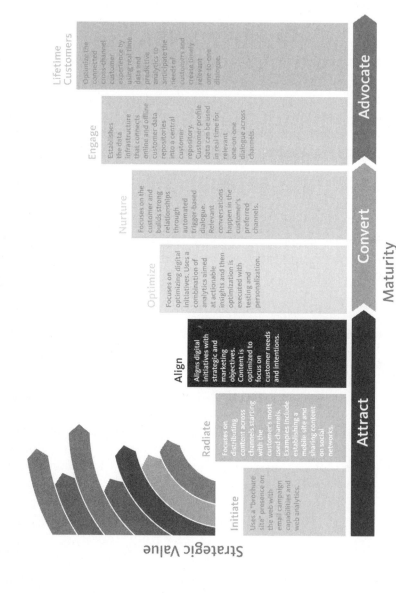

Figure 7.1 Sitecore® Customer Experience Maturity Model™—Align Stage

Objectives of the Align Stage

The main objectives of the Align stage are:

- Show how digital goals drive strategic and marketing objectives.

- Create an Engagement Value Scale (EVS) that values each digital goal according to its relative impact on organizational objectives.

- Define key performance indicators (KPIs) that measure marketing impact and efficiency as well as the relevance to customers.

CASE STORY: FK DISTRIBUTION

What would you do if you were a business that sends out 1.9 million print advertisements twice a week to households and you can see that many of your customers decline them? What pivot would you make to create a highly successful business model? That was the situation facing FK Distribution, a leading print advertising distributor in Denmark. Using creativity and a connected digital experience FK Distribution turned its business model inside out. It now has householders that want its print advertising because it's relevant to their needs.

FK Distribution changed its business model from pushing generic print advertising to a pull model where people receive print advertising that is relevant to their needs. Digital marketing is what makes this possible. Its new model of personalized pull advertising not only meets its customers' personal needs, it meets FK Distribution's core strategic objective of increasing revenue based on the volume of advertisements distributed.

FK Distribution began its transformation by exploring how digital marketing could build a strong connection with the households receiving its ads. Then it built a digital system that aligned customer needs, digital goals, and business objectives. With its old website, it just measured the traditional metrics of visits, page views, and time on site—it gave the company no insight into customer needs. Everyone got the same two inches of paper. In its new digital marketing system it invites householders to complete an online profile of what advertising is relevant to them. FK Distributions now captures customer preferences, profiles, and engagement levels of its customers. Customers can access and update their ad preferences from any device—desktop, mobile, or a custom mobile app—so FK Distribution also knows their preferred channel.

Instead of a declining business of print advertisements, which largely went to trash cans, FK Distribution has built a digital universe. Householders in Denmark are going to the new website and choosing relevant advertisements and special offers available in their local area.

The company estimates that with its old system of generic ads, 30 percent were thrown in the trash without being read. Research now shows that householders who personalize their ad selections are more likely to look through ads because they are relevant. Advertisers also think it's a good idea given that 80 advertisers have signed up so far. And it's great for the environment; a government research council estimates that 30,000 tons of paper and ink will be saved the first year.

The next step for FK Distribution is to give households access to digital advertisements. To do this it has built a mobile app and a dedicated site where householders can select the advertisements and campaigns relevant to them. The app enables visitors to browse through relevant promotions and special offers from a range of retailers instead of having to access each retailer's separate site or online catalog.

This digital transformation has opened new horizons for FK Distribution. It can now connect with householders through the householder's preferred digital channel and deliver advertising through their custom app. This is opening new marketing opportunities using the customer's own data to build more relevant experiences.

FK Distribution's engagement with its customers has shown significant results. As a result of creating a connected customer experience the company is seeing:

- Greater insights about household needs and preferences.

- Improved ties to customers.

- More frequent customer connection with relevant commercials either delivered or accessed weekly through the app.

BENEFITS OF ALIGNING

It's sad to say, but most marketers aren't exactly sure where to put their next marketing dollar. This is especially true in the age of digital marketing and an ever-increasing number of marketing channels and constantly shrinking response rate. In the past marketers were faced with three or four channels—print, television, radio, or outdoor display. Marketers could put enough money into one message and channel and thereby reach a majority of the mass market they wanted to reach.

Broad mass messaging is now a waste of time and resources because there are so many channels to choose from. And individuals can filter when and what topic they want. John Wanamaker, the creator of modern department stores, is credited with saying, "Half the money I spend on advertising is wasted; the problem is that I don't know which half." That problem is even greater now.

Marketers face two very difficult tasks. First, they must align their digital strategy with marketing goals that achieve strategic objectives. When they do this correctly, they can prove with data that their marketing is achieving critical top- and bottom-line objectives. Second, they must create a portfolio of marketing efforts and messages that crosses all of these online and offline channels. The messaging in each channel must complement and strengthen the messages in other channels, and marketers must know which channel is most efficient so they can optimize marketing across the channels. By following the processes described in the previous chapter for the Initiate and Radiate stages you will serve the needs of your customers. And by following the processes described in this chapter for the Align stage you will achieve the objectives of your organization.

Benefits to Your Customers

Marketing must change. In the past marketing has been like a circus barker, yelling the same message louder and louder to throngs of consumers walking by. In most cases marketers have ignored personal interaction with customers and just continued to yell the same broad message. Using this crude method, marketers, at best, convert 1 percent to 2 percent of the customers hearing their message.

Think about how you personally buy or engage with organizations, profit or nonprofit. You, and every other consumer, want a relationship that is relevant to you. You want marketing messages that fit your needs, that target your personality, and that solve your problems. You want someone to whisper a relevant message in your ear, not yell a booming broadcast through a megaphone.

To be most effective as marketers, we have to serve both our customers and our organizational objectives. We must have alignment all the way. We must have marketing that is relevant to our customers, those must be quality customers with a high conversion rate in our digital goals, and those digital goals must be shown to drive organizational objectives. In the case of FK Distribution, the case described at the beginning of this chapter, the company was able to improve the relevance of print advertising to recipients. This increased the value of FK Distribution's services to its end customers, the advertising buyers.

The only way we can create this alignment is to identify how that chain works from customer to objectives and then measure the results we get with our marketing efforts. To do this, we need to create the Strategic Objectives Map and the Experience Analytics described in this chapter.

Aligning also involves the creation of Engagement Values, described later in this chapter. Engagement Values measure the impact a digital goal has on the organizational objectives. An additional outcome is that Engagement Values measure the relevance of a marketing effort to the customer's needs and desires. For example, a campaign or page that has accumulated a high Engagement Value has a high relevance for customers. Alignment produces a win-win relationship between the customer and the organization.

Benefits to Your Organization

To see the business impact that aligning and accurately measuring marketing would have, we only need to look at the revolution that changed manufacturing in the 1990s, the move to enterprise resource planning (ERP). ERP enabled manufacturing companies to track raw material coming into a factory, along with the time, cost, and efficiency at each point in the factory, and continued touch points all the way to customer delivery. The result was a quantum leap in manufacturing production and efficiency.

Using the processes in this book, marketers can create an ERP for marketing. We can measure the impact and efficiency of marketing efforts, we can measure the effect on customers at each touch point, and we can tie them directly to our organizations' strategic and marketing objectives. Marketers can walk into a boardroom and show how and to what degree marketing is driving business objectives.

In FK Distribution this alignment process enabled it to create more relevance for recipients of print advertising by giving recipients a way to identify their preferences. At the same time this alignment met FK Distributions' strategic objectives of creating a business model that stood up to the changes in advertising while providing focused targeting for advertising buyers.

In our assessments with the Sitecore Customer Experience Maturity Assessment of more than 1,000 organizations, 33 percent said their organizations had "KPIs aligned with business objectives," plus "KPIs aligned with CLC across multiple online and offline channels." The other 67 percent are basically marketing by throwing out messages, unsure whether they are relevant to customers and whether they are achieving objectives. We have to change. We have to practice data-driven marketing.

By creating Strategic Objective Maps, like the example later in this chapter, and measuring results with Experience Analytics, your organization can expect to:

- Prove how digital goals and marketing campaigns drive marketing and strategic objectives.

- Measure how relevant your marketing is to customers.

- Identify which channels and campaigns are most valuable and efficient for specific customer segments or personas.

- Validate a match between content/assets and the segment or persona they were created for.

- Measure marketing efficiency by channel, which gives us a way to balance our cross-channel portfolio.

What You Need to Do to Align

A successful marketer can show the CEO and board exactly how marketing drives success in strategic and marketing objectives. Obviously, to do that you must first identify your organization's strategic objectives and the marketing objectives that drive them. It doesn't matter whether your organization is a for-profit, nonprofit, B2B, B2C, or government. This process has worked in all types of organizations.

There are six steps to creating the Strategic Objectives Map that links your digital goals to strategic and marketing objectives. Figure 7.2 shows the six steps.

Figure 7.2 Six Steps to Aligning Marketing Actions with Organizational Strategy

How to Align Marketing with Strategic Objectives

When you complete the following process you will have a causal map that shows how digital goals in your digital channels drive marketing objectives, which in turn achieve strategic objectives. (Digital goals are the goals or conversions that customers complete on the website—for example, registering on the website for a newsletter.) Figure 7.3 shows an example of a Strategic Objectives Map connecting digital goals to a strategic theme.

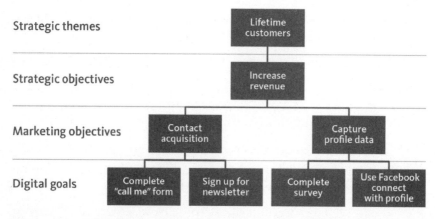

Figure 7.3 Map Connecting Digital Goals to Strategic Theme

Digital goals are the interactions or conversions that customers complete on the website—for example, registering on the site for a newsletter or filling in a trip calculator. The customer's actions and behavior in completing a digital goal move the visitor closer to the marketing objective.

Most organizations have two or at most three complementary strategic themes. You can usually recognize these themes immediately. A few examples of strategic themes are highest quality, customer intimacy, lowest-cost provider, or total solution. For example, Lexus has a strategic theme of highest quality. Nordstrom is recognized for knowing its customers—customer intimacy. What two or three strategic themes is your organization recognized for? A list of the most recognized themes follows in the next subsection.

Once you know your organization's strategic themes, you need to identify the strategic objectives that make those themes a reality. It's the way you execute your objectives that creates differentiation from other companies. Strategic objectives can include increasing revenue, decreasing costs, increasing customer satisfaction, expanding geographic distribution, increasing brand awareness, or increasing new product development and promotion. Strategic objectives are not just about marketing. They include objectives from all business functions.

Marketing objectives are objectives the marketing team executes to support strategic objectives. Two examples of marketing objectives are increasing marketing qualified leads (MQLs) and capturing customer data.

Identifying Strategic Themes

The first step is to identify the two or three strategic themes that are the foundation of your organization's strategy. Strategic themes are broad statements of how the company expects to succeed.

There are a limited number of strategic themes used in organizations, no matter what their business model is or whether they are profit or nonprofit. The following table lists some of the strategic themes and examples of companies using those themes. Additional strategic themes for nonprofit and government organizations are on this book's associated website www.ConnectTheExperience.com/strategicthemes.

Common Strategic Themes

Theme	Company	Description
Quality	Lexus, BMW	Products or services are recognized as having the highest quality.
Innovation	Intel, Apple	Products are the most innovative and advanced in the company's industry or segment.
Total solution	IBM	Provide everything needed by the customer. In the case of IBM this is hardware, software, consulting, and support.
Operational efficiency	Dell, General Electric	Manufacturing, operations, and distribution are vastly superior to competitors.
Lowest cost	Walmart	Initial cost of purchase is the lowest.
Expand the franchise	McDonald's, Starbucks	Increase the number of outlets to meet the customer at every possible location.
Customer intimacy	Lands' End	Know the customer's needs so well marketers can make recommendations visitors appreciate.
Total value	Walmart	The sum of total benefits for the customer beats all competitors.
System lock-in	Microsoft, Oracle	Once you start with this company's products or services, it is very difficult to switch to a competitor.
Corporate citizenship	Procter & Gamble, Vodafone, Whole Foods	Stand out as the leader in corporate and social responsibility in legal, ethical, environmental, and community areas.
Niche	WD-40 Company	Small vertical, functional, or geographic market that can be differentiated, focused on, and defended.

Theme	Company	Description
Exclusive image	Gucci	Perceived image implies exclusivity, but not necessarily quality.
Blue sky	Cirque du Soleil	Combines two or more existing businesses into a completely new business in an untapped market.
Disintermediation	Zappos.com, Amazon.com	Remove the middleman.
Aggregator/hub	Lawyers.com	Trusted matchmaker and escrow agent who knows everyone on both sides and makes matches that wouldn't happen otherwise. (Secret knowledge that isn't publicly available is critical.)

What to Do

Write down the two or three strategic themes that state the direction for your organization. This is an excellent exercise to conduct with a group of experienced managers. If necessary, operational managers may want to do interviews at the vice president level to learn the executive-level view of strategic theme and organizational objectives.

Themes should be complementary; for example, a niche theme and customer intimacy strengthen each other. Conversely, innovation and lowest cost are themes that would be difficult for a start-up in a new market to execute simultaneously.

Keep the names of your strategic themes brief—two or three words. You can select from themes in the preceding list, choose from the nonprofit and government themes on the companion website, or create your own. (See www.ConnectTheExperience.com/strategicthemes.)

Identifying Strategic Objectives

Although there are only a few strategic themes, there are many objectives that can be used to achieve a theme. For your organization to create strategic themes successfully, you will have to execute strategic objectives across many business functions. Your strategic objectives and how well you execute them are what differentiate your organization from your competitors.

Strategic objectives cross many business units such as sales, distribution, and manufacturing. Although these are all important you are probably most familiar with marketing.

What to Do

Create a tree diagram or table with your most important strategic themes at the top. There are usually one or two and never more than three. Under each theme write the two or three strategic objectives that must be executed for the strategic theme to be successful. If you are only familiar with how marketing can contribute to success, then skip to the next step.

Let's take as an example the strategic theme to increase shareholder value. In this case, the strategic objectives to accomplish this could be:

Theme	Strategic Objective
Increase shareholder value	Increase revenue
	Increase depth into existing market segments
	Increase lifetime value of customers

Identifying Marketing Objectives

Every marketer should understand their company's marketing objectives—how marketing objectives drive success in the strategic objectives.

Most for-profit organizations with existing products and services will have "increase marketing qualified leads" (MQLs) as one of their top marketing objectives. Most nonprofit organizations will have an equivalent marketing objective of increase retention, increase donations, or increase advocacy. There are many other supporting marketing objectives.

What to Do

Using a tree structure or a table like the preceding one, follow two steps:

1. Write one to three of the most important marketing objectives that drive strategic objectives. If one of the strategic objectives is internal, such as "reduce manufacturing costs," then it may not have a marketing objective. Use a verb-modifier-noun format, as this is often helpful.

2. It may be best to work with just your top marketing objectives. This will help keep your later work focused. However, you may find that the digital goals you select in the next step drive multiple marketing objectives.

To continue the previous example, with a theme such as increase shareholder value and its strategic objectives, there are many marketing objectives that could be used. The mix of marketing objectives you choose depends on the other themes you want to achieve, your existing organization, culture, capabilities, and so on.

Theme	Strategic Objective	Marketing Objective
Increase shareholder value	Increase revenue	Increase marketing qualified leads (MQLs)
		Increase quality of lead and deal size
	Increase lifetime value of customers	Increase knowledge of customer needs, behavior, and decision journey
		Increase recaptured and repeat business

Identifying Digital Goals That Drive Marketing Objectives

In the following process you will identify digital goals that drive your marketing objectives. (As described earlier, digital goals are the interactions or conversions that customers complete on the website—for example, registering on the site for a newsletter or filling in a trip calculator.) These digital goals could be in any digital channel such as social, mobile app, or email.

An important point to recognize here is that not all digital goals are equal in their impact on achieving your marketing objectives. For example, registering for a newsletter does not have the same impact on revenue as completing a form to have a salesperson call or demonstrate the product.

Think of the digital goals that help your customers move through the stages in their decision journey. Can you use a simple registration form during the acquisition stage? Can you use an iterative registration during research asking for an additional piece of data each time they download? Will an online calculator or product configurator enable them to find what they want and help you understand their needs? At what stage do they compare products? Are there nurturing sequences that use goals as gates between each stage? What digital goal signifies they are ready to commit?

The possibilities for digital goals are rapidly expanding. Where there used to be simple newsletter registration forms, there are now online calculators that capture visitor preferences and future needs, social games that network in new visitors, highly personalized goals targeting specific personas, and far more. You need to brainstorm the digital goals that will attract your highest-quality visitors, nurture them to greater commitment, and accelerate them through the decision journey.

There are different types of goals: transactional goals, informational goals, and process goals. While transactional goals show the greatest engagement, the other two types of goals can also be used if there are few transaction goals in your marketing. These can be described as:

- *Transactional goal.* Transactional goals usually involve two-way communication and an exchange of information.

- *Informational goal.* Informational goals are one-way transfers of information that involve little risk, like downloading a free white paper without registering. These have low risk and should have low value.

- *Process goal.* Process goals involve multiple actions by the customer. This could be, for example, requiring a marketing qualified lead to complete steps such as downloading an asset, subscribing to an email, and requesting a phone call.

Now that you have clear marketing objectives, you need to brainstorm digital goals for all your channels that will help you achieve your objectives. Brainstorming these goals is best done by a group of experienced marketers. And if you've tried brainstorming and it didn't work, then try the brainstorming method described in the book's companion website www.ConnectTheExperience.com/checklists.

Too often brainstorming produces only the loudest person's ideas or the highest-paid person's opinion (HIPPO). The method described on the companion website is one that produces the best and most diverse set of goals. When you have completed your brainstorming, you should have sets of digital goals that you can implement immediately and sets you can stage for future development.

What to Do

The book's companion website contains a checklist that will help you lead your team to generate digital goals to achieve your marketing objectives: www.ConnectTheExperience.com/checklists.

After identifying your top digital goals and categories, you might have a table of digital goal categories that looks like this:

Theme	Strategic Objective	Marketing Objective	Digital Goal Category
Increase shareholder value	Increase revenue	Increase marketing qualified leads (MQLs)	Responding to email registration
		Increase quality of leads and deal size	Completion of "Call Me" forms
	Increase lifetime value of customers	Increase knowledge of customer needs, behavior, and decision journey	Completion of incremental registrations to capture more data
			Joining "Loyalty Member Club"

Every group we lead through this exercise has found it stimulating and exciting. Most digital goals will aggregate into about six groups. These groups of digital goals will be assigned an Engagement Value in the next section of this chapter. That Engagement Value will later become a proxy for achieving your strategic objective, for example, to increase revenue.

WHAT YOU NEED TO DO TO MEASURE IMPACT AND ALIGNMENT

Once you have identified the digital goals that drive your marketing objectives, you need an estimate of the digital goal's impact on your strategic and marketing objectives. The measure of the impact on the objective is also a measure of the customer's engagement. That measure is known as the Engagement Value. The Engagement Value of a digital goal is a relative number that correlates with achieving the strategic and marketing objective.

When you analyze marketing efforts using the Engagement Value metric, you can see which traffic channels, campaigns, pages, assets, and social media have the greatest visitor engagement and relevance. It shows you which are most efficient and have the greatest impact on your strategic and marketing objectives.

What Is Engagement Value?

Engagement Value answers the most important question for marketing, "Which conversions are most important to achieving strategic and marketing objectives?" In traditional web analytics all conversions have the same weight. But every marketer knows not all conversions are equal. For an e-commerce company, registering for a newsletter does not have the same impact on the company's strategic objectives of revenue as completing a purchase. For a nonprofit, registering for a webinar does not have the same impact as a donation. Engagement Values can be developed for all types of organizations, but one of the easiest business models in which to understand Engagement Value is in e-commerce. In a simplified example, an e-commerce business could have digital goals of,

- Add to basket
- Add to wish list

- Sign up for offer
- Order completion

Obviously these digital goals do not contribute equally to achieving the organization's strategic objective of increasing revenue. Order completion is a direct driver of the strategic objective. Initially a team of marketers can estimate how much each digital goal contributes to achieving revenue. By applying a mathematical correlation we can assign weights to each digital goal. In this example appropriate weights might be:

Digital Goal	Engagement Value
Add to basket	1
Add to wish list	2
Sign up for offer	20
Order completion	100

Digital goals and Engagement Values can be created for all business models whether they are profit, nonprofit, government, or any type. The important thing is that each Engagement Value must be proportional to how much each digital goal contributes to achieving the strategic objective. Examples of Engagement Value Scales for different organizations are at www.ConnectTheExperience.com/EVS.

What Is an Engagement Value Scale?

Figure 7.4 shows the Engagement Value Scale (EVS) for a B2B business that has a long sales cycle with a strategic objective of increasing revenue. From bottom to top, digital goals are weighted according to their level of impact on achieving strategic objectives. The value of each level should be proportional to how much that level contributes to the customer achieving the strategic objective. (This book's companion website contains multiple examples of Engagement Value Scales for many types of businesses, both profit and nonprofit.)

The labels on the left are the categories of digital goals. These groups will be different depending on your marketing objectives and your organization's type of business. For example, if you are a nonprofit with activism as one of your key objectives, then your top goals might

Request call — 100

Request pricing — 50

Request for white paper — 25

Sign up for webinar — 10

Register for newsletter — 5

Watch short video
View page — 0

Figure 7.4   B2B Engagement Value Scale Showing the Relative Impact of Each Digital Goal on the Marketing Objectives

be volunteering or donations. If you are an e-commerce organization, it would be completing the purchase.

Not all digital goals have the same value. Looking at a web page without registering requires no communication or risk exchange, so it has no value. Registering for a newsletter with an email address requires a small amount of trust between the customer and the site owner. However, asking for a salesperson to call your personal phone number represents a high level of commitment and has a high Engagement Value.

Experience Analytics Complements Traditional Analytics

Traditional web analytics records metrics based on technical quantitative data. It doesn't record visitor behavior. This is because traditional web analytics works on the data from log files, data like time on page, page views, and so on. These are not valid measures of how engaged visitors are, and they are not valid measures of how well your marketing impacts your organizational objectives because they only measure quantity of interactions and not their quality. To measure visitor engagement across channels we need a different metric, Engagement Value.

Experience Analytics, the analysis of Engagement Value, records the visitor's behavior and is a more accurate judgment of visitor intent than traditional web analytics. Using Experience Analytics, you are able to evaluate how much each channel, campaign, asset, and page contributes toward achieving the strategic and marketing objective.

Experience Analytics is the analysis of marketing's relevance and the impact on strategic and marketing objectives. Experience Analytics uses Engagement Value as the primary metric. Marketing efficiency can be derived from Engagement Value and the number of visits that produced the Engagement Value.

With traditional analytics it is very difficult to compare marketing impact or efficiency across channels. With Experience Analytics the same metric is used across all channels, so comparisons of impact and efficiency are straightforward. This makes Experience Analytics a great tool for balancing a cross-channel marketing portfolio.

What to Do

When you develop the Engagement Value Scale, you should involve the most important and most experienced stakeholders. You need their buy-in, their influence on others, and most importantly their cross-functional experience in selecting and weighting the most important goals.

The team you bring together should have 8 to 12 people who are highly experienced in marketing or digital marketing. Some examples of team members might be:

- Chief marketing officer or CMO representative
- Customer engagement/brand manager
- Channel managers
- Analysts
- E-commerce marketers
- Sales

- Agency

- Information technology (IT)

Additional roles you may want to include on your team are described in Chapter 12.

To create an Engagement Value Scale, you and your team will create a rank-ordered list with the most impactful goal at the top and the least impactful goal at the bottom. Rank the highest goal as 100 and the lowest 0, and then assign proportional values to the goals in between.

The book's companion website contains checklists and tips guiding your team in creating the Engagement Value Scale. Check the companion website at www.ConnectTheExperience.com/checklists.

Warning! Optimizing using Engagement Values optimizes your marketing to improve those goals that have an Engagement Value. This means that if you place Engagement Value on the wrong goals you will optimize your marketing to improve those wrong goals. This happens most frequently when marketers set Engagement Value on page search, log-ins, viewing a page, partial completion of a purchase funnel, or watching a generic video.

WHAT YOU NEED TO DO WITH EXPERIENCE ANALYTICS

Experience Analytics enables you to measure your marketing's impact and effectiveness in achieving your marketing objectives. Experience Analytics begins in Stage 3, Align. Here are some examples of Experience Analytics that aren't available with traditional web analytics.

Measuring Marketing Impact and Effectiveness with Value and Value per Visit

Engagement Value is a measure of how much value a channel, campaign, page, or asset has contributed toward achieving strategic objectives. As customers complete (convert) digital goals, they accumulate in their visitor record the total value of all digital goals they have converted. As visitors pass through channels, campaigns, pages, or assets, the system tracks the value of all passing visitors. In that way you can see the total value of all visitors who have passed through a channel, campaign, web page, or asset. Those channels, campaigns, pages, or assets that have had a lot of high-value visitors pass through them have a high impact on objectives. One of the simplest yet most valuable reports shows the channels, campaigns, web pages, or assets that have generated the highest value (see Figure 7.5).

Engagement Value is a powerful metric, but there's more we can do with it. Just as you measure the fuel efficiency of your car with miles per gallon, we can measure marketing efficiency with Value per Visit.

Value per Visit is a measure of how much value was produced for the number of visitors. You can use it to compare efficiency across marketing channels, to compare campaign efficiency, or to compare the relevance of a page to visitors.

Value per Visits is also a measure of customer relevance. If you send a campaign to both Persona A and Persona B, but Persona B produces a higher Value per Visit, you know it was more relevant to Persona B.

Balancing Impact and Effectiveness across Channels

Engagement Value and Value per Visit are also great ways to balance your marketing efforts across multiple channels (see Figure 7.6). With traditional web analytics the metrics for each channel are different so you end up trying to compare apples and pelicans. However, with Experience Analytics you can compare different channels or subchannels using the same metrics, Value and Value per Visit. For example, you can compare the Engagement Value and Value per Visit of an email campaign promoting a webinar against a pay-per-click (PPC) ad for an e-book.

Marketing Impact and Effectiveness by Campaign or Asset

With Experience Analytics it's obvious which campaigns or assets produce the total greatest impact; just look at the Engagement Value for a campaign or asset, as shown in Figure 7.7. To see the effectiveness, look at the Value per Visit for a campaign or asset. Traditional web analytics identifies campaigns that produce the most visitors, but they

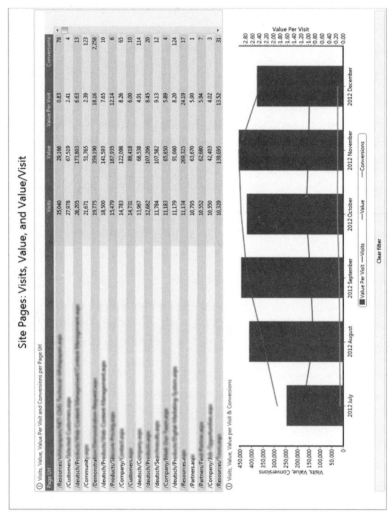

Figure 7.5 A Simple but Powerful Report Shows Which Pages Have the Highest Value and Impact on Objectives

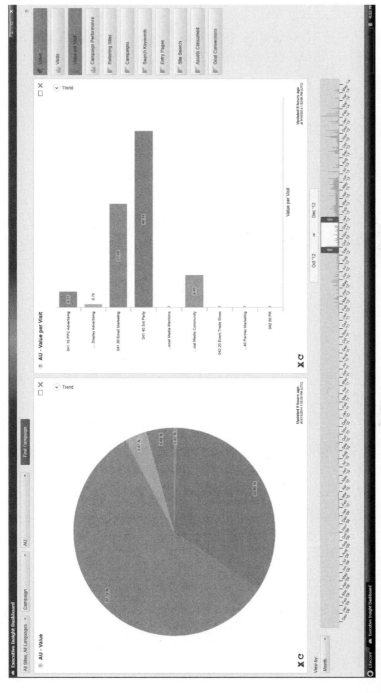

Figure 7.6 Use Value per Visit to Compare Marketing Impact and Efficiency in Different Channels

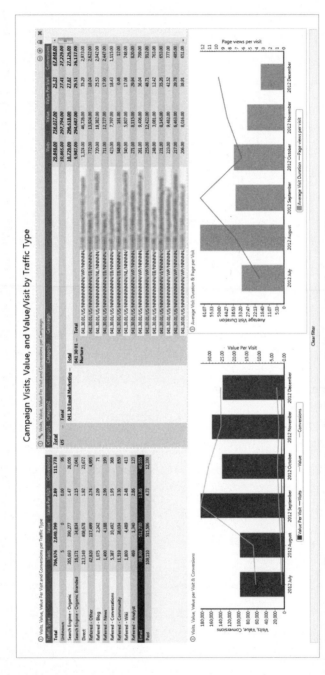

Figure 7.7   Campaigns Sorted by Visits and Showing Value and Value per Visit

can't help you identify the campaigns that produce the highest-quality (highest-value) customers. Experience Analytics shows you which campaigns produce the most impact, Value, and which have the highest efficiency, Value per Visit.

Experience Analytics becomes even more important when analyzing your marketing's value and effectiveness by visitor segment or persona.

Improving Campaign Performance with the Marketing Optimization Matrix

Most marketers face the task of improving hundreds, if not thousands, of campaigns. With that many campaigns to sort through, marketers need to use the Sitecore® Marketing Optimization Matrix (MOM) to help them decide which campaigns are the best to leverage and repeat and which campaigns can be optimized with a small amount of work. The MOM shows a campaign's impact and identifies how it can be improved to optimize your marketing.

A good MOM should help marketers answer questions such as:

- Which campaigns produce the greatest impact and should be repeated and leveraged?

- Which campaigns could be great with a few small changes?

- What change is needed to move a specific campaign from good to great?

- Which campaign will give the most marginal improvement for a small effort?

The Four Quadrants of MOM

The Marketing Optimization Matrix has four quadrants: Heroes, Converters, Attractors, and Nulls, as shown in Figure 7.8.

Each dot in the MOM is a specific campaign. The vertical axis (Y-axis) is the Engagement Value a campaign produces. The horizontal axis (X-axis) is the number of visits for a campaign. The location of a campaign in the matrix shows you how much impact the campaign has and how you can improve that campaign.

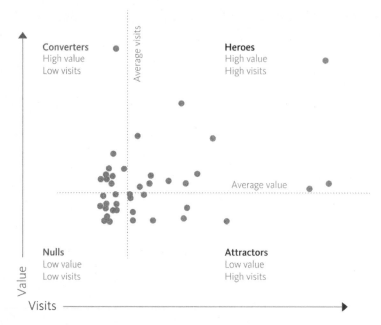

Figure 7.8   Sitecore® Marketing Optimization Matrix

The vertical dashed line running parallel to the left-hand axis in the MOM chart is the average number of visits. The horizontal dashed line running parallel to the bottom axis is the average value. All campaigns above the horizontal line are above average in Engagement Value. All campaigns to the right of the vertical line are above average in visits.

Heroes, in the top right quadrant, produce high Engagement Value and a high number of visits. That means high marketing impact. Hero campaigns should be repeated and leveraged as much as possible.

Converters, in the top left quadrant, convert well, but they don't attract many visitors. They need their attractiveness increased. A list of best practices for increasing attraction can tell us what the best actions are for improving campaigns in the Converter quadrant.

Attractors, in the lower right quadrant, attract a lot of visits, but they don't convert well. They need their conversion rate increased. A list of best practices for increasing conversion can tell us what to change to increase attraction.

Nulls, in the lower left quadrant, either have run only a short time or are not doing well. Most often they are a waste of marketing resources. If a Nulls campaign has run long enough that it should have produced results, then you should stop the campaign and put your marketing efforts elsewhere.

MOM Helps Marketers Take Action

What is very important about MOM is that each quadrant helps marketers decide what action to take to optimize their digital marketing:

- Heroes should be repeated and leveraged.

- Attractors should have their conversion rate increased.

- Converters should have their attractiveness increased.

- Nulls should be stopped.

The chart shown in Figure 7.9 gives a few best practices for improving a campaign depending upon the quadrant in which it falls.

The quadrant in which a campaign appears in the Marketing Optimization Matrix identifies the action marketers should take to optimize their marketing. For additional tips on how marketers can take action to improve campaigns using MOM, refer to the companion website for this book www.ConnectTheExperience.com/mom.

	Low Visits	High Visits

High Value	**Converters**
	Increase Attractiveness
	• Captivating title
	• Keywords at front of titles and subtitles
	• Aligned title, landing page, content
	• Segment target audience
	• Banner placement
	• Pro layout and artwork
	• A/B, MV test
		Heroes
		Repeat and Leverage
		• Leverage topic to other media and channels
		• Repeat use of title/topic in
		  • Overview
		  • Detailed
		  • Niche or Vertical
		• Segment by demographic, psychographic, geographic
		• A/B, MV test

Low Value	**Nulls** Delete Them • Run long enough to test • Delete	**Attractors** **Increase Conversions** • Strong and repeated Call To Actions • More valuable offer • More attractive label on Submit button • Test web form • Check funnel abandonment • A/B, MV test

Figure 7.9 Best Practices for Digital Marketing

ADDITIONAL WAYS TO INCREASE ALIGNMENT

Aligning an organization for maximum impact goes far beyond aligning digital goals with organization objectives. An organization that is focused on a few objectives and in alignment has magnitudes more power than an organization where each silo has a separate focus and none are aligned. It is not within marketing's power to bring your whole organization into alignment, but here are some ways that marketing can continue to benefit from alignment.

Aligning to Increase Acquisition Marketing

Almost every organization has increasing new customer acquisition as one of its primary business objectives. Once you have implemented an Engagement Value Scale, you can evaluate your channels, campaign topics, keywords, and visitor segments to learn where your marketing has the greatest impact and efficiency. With this knowledge you learn at Stage 3 that you can be more cost-effective with online retargeting and display advertising.

Aligning with Sales

As you gather more knowledge in Stage 3, you can begin to feed leads and customer insights to your sales teams. If you are using a digital marketing system that captures the online actions of individual visitors, then you can begin to identify marketing qualified leads (MQLs). Although this is much more effective in Stage 6 when customer relationship management (CRM) and customer data are linked, the process of lead generation can begin here. With marketing systems that track individual visitor action you can pass the visitor's interest and history to sales. For example, in a B2B business before passing a high volume of leads to sales, marketing and sales need to work closely to define marketing qualified leads (MQLs) and sales accepted leads (SALs). Similarly, in a B2C business a call center agent could review all of a visitor's interactions and interests before contacting them.

If your marketing data aggregates all visitors, then you won't have data on specific online visitors. However, you can pass data from registered visitors to sales if they have completed a detailed registration. You can also brief sales on insights from aggregate data such as changes in product interest in specific regions, and new customer segments.

Aligning Customer Intelligence throughout Your Organization

Often the first changes in customer preferences, sentiment, and behavior are visible through digital channels. When marketers detect changes in customer behavior, they should brief other departments that might be effected. For example, changes in social sentiment should alert the public relations department. Changes on Yelp or other ratings services should inform support, warranty, and service departments. These are all new voices of the customer, and marketing hears these voices first through the digital channels.

BREAKING BARRIERS

Stakeholders are quick to get on board with aligning digital goals, marketing objectives, and strategic objectives. Everyone wants a clear picture of how they contribute to the greater objective of the organization. However, the Align stage can become more difficult during the technical implementation of the Engagement Value Scale and Experience Analytics.

If you have an analytics solution that is designed to use an Engagement Value, then it is very straightforward to begin entering Engagement Values immediately for each goal. We have had workshops where the client began entering Engagement Values on goals the day after the workshop, began gathering data that week, and within two weeks had data it could use to drive business decisions.

If you do not have an analytics solution that is robust enough for Experience Analytics, then you will need to work with IT and your analysts to develop a workable system. In some cases, it could be as simple as entering goals and accepting that your Engagement Values will be used only to compare cross-channel marketing. (That's still a great win.) With other systems it may require training and additional software that installs additional code on goals so value can be tracked.

Once your system is capturing Engagement Values, you can use the vendor's analytics tool, Microsoft Excel, Tableau, or another data visualization tool to develop reports and dashboards like those described earlier in this chapter.

Barriers can arise in the Align stage with the people who should most embrace the change. Analysts who have dedicated themselves to learning arcane and difficult-to-use analytic tools may feel that Experience Analytics detracts from their expertise. They have spent years learning how to make a subjective judgment on engagement based on page views, bounce rates, and click-through rates. Now, those years of experience and subjective judgment might have less value with the use of Experience Analytics.

Analysts should look at Experience Analytics as a way of reducing their workload with daily analytics, and begin looking at how they can contribute at a more strategic level. When analysts do have additional time, they can use it to balance cross-channel marketing, develop personas and segments, and search out answers to ad hoc questions and new markets. These are all fields of analytic exploration that are more exciting and valuable.

MOVING TO A HIGHER LEVEL OF MARKETING

In the space of two meetings you can map your digital goals and marketing objectives. Another meeting and you have your Engagement Value Scale. Checklists and tips on conducting these meetings are available on this book's companion website www.ConnectTheExperience .com/checklists.

The introduction of Experience Analytics will give you a better handle on what marketing efforts produce the greatest value. Using Experience Analytics to do this requires less analytic skill than traditional web analytics, but it does require an expanded view of analytics, so your analysts and channel managers will need to learn the concepts of Engagement Value and Experience Analytics.

Most organizations find that moving from traditional analytics to Experience Analytics requires a period of adjustment as they gain trust in the new numbers. It's like riding a bike with training wheels and then having the training wheels removed. Once the training wheels are removed, you begin to learn that they were actually a restraint and made cornering, speed, and agility more difficult.

KNOWING YOU HAVE ARRIVED

How do you know when you've arrived at the Align stage? What will change once you have aligned digital goals with strategic and marketing objectives and you begin using Experience Analytics?

A lot of business insights and management visibility and rewards begin at this stage. Your marketing objectives are transparent and well-defined. That means marketing employees have a clear understanding of what marketing objectives are and how they personally impact the organization's objectives. That can be very empowering and motivating. It also does away with clutter.

Reporting focuses on business objectives, not on technical web metrics. This makes executives and managers aware of marketing's impact on business. Executive reports now show impact on business objectives and actionable issues rather than focusing on traditional web analytics metrics like visits, time on page, and bounce rate.

Channel portfolio management becomes easier once you employ Engagement Values on your digital goals. You can use Engagement Value to gauge the impact each channel produces and Value per Visit to gauge the channel's marketing efficiency. For example, if you see a channel with high efficiency but low value, you will probably want to put more marketing effort into it.

Experience analytics is accessible to all marketers, not just analysts. Channel and campaign managers can do day-to-day analytics necessary for channel balancing and performance improvement when they use Engagement Value and Value per Visit. Daily analytics do not need the interpretation of an analyst. This gives analysts more time to investigate new marketing insights.

It is easier to validate content and campaigns for specific visitor segments or personas. Experience Analytics makes it easy to see whether content or campaigns targeting a specific persona or customer segment achieved high value. If you see that a campaign or downloadable asset has a high value for one specific visitor segment or persona, then you know exactly where to target your marketing and increase attraction.

Campaign managers using the Marketing Optimization Matrix (MOM) will find it easier to identify campaigns they should repeat and leverage. MOM also shows them what type of changes to make to improve marginal campaigns.

CHAPTER 8

Stage 4—Optimize

If you're trying to persuade people to do something, or buy something, it seems to me you should use their language.

—David Ogilvy

O rganizations in this stage focus on optimizing digital initiatives. This stage uses a combination of analytics aimed at actionable insights and optimization using testing and personalization (see Figure 8.1).

THE OPTIMIZE STAGE

Going to the Optimize stage marks an important shift of focus. The focus shifts from marketing tactics to acquire traffic to focusing on how to optimize the experience and how to achieve your objectives.

The first step in optimizing is to change one-size-fits-all messaging to messaging tailored to unique customer segments, their needs, motivations, and objectives. Personalization is key to this. It enables you to create better and more targeted conversations. As we cover in this chapter, personalization comes in many flavors. In the Optimize stage, your focus will be on quick wins using the easier methods of personalization.

The next important step in optimizing is to focus on digital goals that are key to achieving your strategic objectives. Creating better experiences through personalization is not only a win for the

Customer Experience Maturity Model

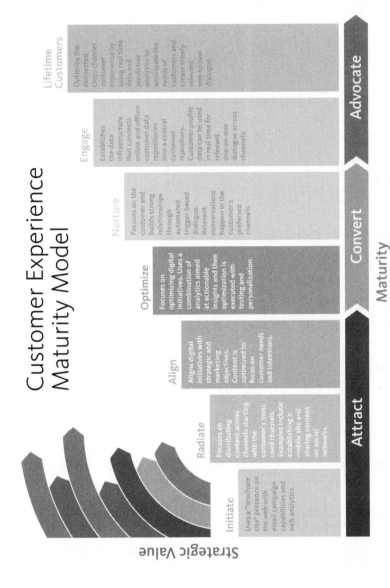

Initiate
Uses a "brochure site" presence on the web with email campaign capabilities and web analytics.

Radiate
Focuses on distributing content across channels starting with the customer's most used channels. Examples include establishing a mobile site and sharing content on social networks.

Align
Aligns digital initiatives with strategic and marketing objectives. Content is optimized to focus on customer needs and intentions.

Optimize
Focuses on optimizing digital initiatives. Uses a combination of analytics aimed at actionable insights and then optimization is executed with testing and personalization.

Nurture
Focuses on the customer and builds strong relationships through automated trigger-based dialogue. Relevant conversations happen in the customer's preferred channels.

Engage
Establishes the data infrastructure that connects online and offline customer data repositories into a central customer repository. Customer profile data can be used in real time for relevant one-on-one dialogue across channels.

Lifetime Customers
Optimize the connected cross-channel customer experience by using real time data and predictive analytics to anticipate the needs of customers and create timely relevant one-to-one dialogue.

Strategic Value

Attract — Convert — Advocate

Maturity

Figure 8.1 Sitecore® Customer Experience Maturity Model™—Optimize Stage

customers, but also for your organization as more engaged customers convert more digital goals. You will also use testing, beginning with A/B testing to optimize conversions. In both personalization and testing Engagement Value will be used to measure which marketing efforts produce the best customer experience and outcomes.

A third area of optimizing is using Engagement Value combined with a marketing taxonomy to optimize marketing initiatives and spend.

Optimizing is a fun journey; it's halfway between one-size-fits-all messaging and the automated personalized messaging. It's the stage where opportunities and gold mines open, all from a few new marketing processes. When optimizing begins to produce its results you will see a new appreciation for the impact marketing can have on strategic objectives.

Objectives of the Optimize Stage

The main objectives of the Optimize stage are:

- Optimize your digital presence to get higher engagement by focusing on the customer first and creating relevant experiences in the different channels used. Use personalization and testing to help learn what is most effective and relevant for the different customers.

- Optimize marketing initiatives by measuring marketing performance across channels.

- Key performance indicators (KPIs) are tied with strategic objectives and measured toward specific marketing objectives.

CASE STORY: QT MUTUAL BANK

How does a bank with a track record for innovation vie for new customers and greater share of wallets in a highly competitive consumer banking market? The answer for QT Mutual Bank (QTMB) was to combine web-based gamification with social media, email, mobile, and data-driven marketing. This helped the bank to create connected customer experiences and achieve a 60 percent increase in quarterly sales growth.

Australia-based QT Mutual Bank offers savings accounts, home loans, credit cards, and financial planning services. With its origins as the Queensland Teachers Credit Union, the bank has a reputation for using technology to magnify its personal banking service. One example is the fact that QTMB was the first financial institution in Australia to install a network of 24-hour ATMs in 1977. In 2011, QTMB became one of Australia's first mutual banks.

Facing an increasingly competitive atmosphere, QTMB looked for innovative ways to serve the community while attracting new customers. With a product range that puts it squarely in competition with a number of other banks, a key objective was to enable QTMB to engage its customers in as personal a conversation as they'd have in a branch—whether they're interacting with QTMB's main website, mobile site, or through social media.

The innovative approach that QTMB and its digital agency developed is a campaign called "Staffroom for Improvement." It is an annual campaign that awards a cash prize to a deserving school. The prize is used to refurbish the teachers' staff room of the winning school. The campaign was active for three weeks and open to anyone who registered. A gamification concept encouraged people to return, vote daily, and share with their friends. Participants used apples as virtual "apples for the teacher" that functioned as votes.

Participants were allowed to vote once per day but different techniques were used to generate repeated daily voting. For example, a participant's giving power could be boosted by participating in "happy hours." Participants could also reach higher levels—from Apple Noob to Apple Ninja to Apple Wizard—that would give them increased giving power. A variety of data-driven personalization techniques were used to visually inform logged-in participants about their current giving power.

The Staffroom for Improvement campaign was promoted in QTMB branches, on QTMB.com.au, on the bank's Facebook page, and with a television ad. QTMB's marketers emailed the bank's 70,000 member customers and people who had voted in the previous contest. Visitors where directed to a registration site where a personalized experience helped create context. Results for the campaign were impressive:

60 percent increase in quarterly sales growth

40,000 participants

37,000 survey responses

1.74 million apples (votes) given

7,000 Facebook "likes"

1.25 million-plus Facebook impressions

Collecting and connecting data was an important objective for the campaign. Surveys that QTMB sent out at various timed intervals asked participants about their banking needs. These surveys, supported via email-delivered calls to action, were based on personalization rules such as the recipient's date of birth or home ownership status. For example, a participant born in 1998 would receive a survey asking if they had a savings account, while a survey sent to a married person born in 1978 would inquire about mortgage and credit card needs.

The annual campaign has enabled QTMB to take steps toward forming the QTMB marketer's single view of the customer. Information collected via the different channels provided marketers at QTMB with massive amounts of data. That data was used to personalize the customer experience in the weeks and months following "Staffroom for Improvement." For example, upon returning to the QTMB site, a contest participant who'd provided credit card product information would be greeted with a page comparing the visitor's current card to one of QTMB's three MasterCard products.

This journey for QTMB—where it has moved up the Customer Experience Maturity Model—is a demonstration of how organizations can drive successful business outcomes.

BENEFITS

Moving from the Align stage to the Optimize stage is a prime opportunity for many organizations. It is a chance to shift gears and change focus from pure attraction marketing to optimizing your customers' experience.

Benefits to Your Customers

We all know the feeling when the joy of making a purchase turns to dissatisfaction and frustration. Imagine you have just bought a new TV online. You receive it and when you go to look for some setup information on the site where it was purchased, you see everything but the TV. You probably ask yourself, "Why doesn't the site know that I just bought a TV through this site?" After browsing to the section with the TV, you find that now it's on sale at 10 percent below the price you paid. You still can't find the information you came for, and, to top it off, you are very frustrated at having paid more. You tried to call the number on the screen to get the discount, but end up waiting 20 minutes before being connected to a support representative who tells you he can't give you the discount. And if you want the setup information you originally came back for, then you have to go to the manufacturer's website. By that time the transient joy of buying another electronic gizmo is a distant memory that has been replaced with the strong feeling you will never purchase from this retailer again.

This type of customer interaction is exactly what the Optimize stage is designed to prevent. The Optimize stage is where the customer is at the center. The different interactions customers have with the brand, even across different channels, need to be connected and relevant.

The benefits for the customer are reducing friction and noise and creating relevant connected experiences, something most customers prefer. A survey found that 62 percent of consumers find personalized retail websites useful when shopping online.[1]

Benefits to Your Organization

Moving to the Optimize stage means that you have a clear alignment of strategic objectives, marketing objectives, and digital goals. As the results of optimizing begin to show, a new culture is fostered that is more data driven and focused on achieving key objectives.

Another benefit in the Optimize stage is being more efficient in how you do marketing. As you begin to measure and optimize marketing initiatives, it becomes easier to make better decisions in terms of marketing spend and using past insights to strengthen initiatives or launch new ones.

WHAT YOU NEED TO DO

Optimizing is the process of making your marketing message more relevant to the customer's needs and context. To do this you will need to know the customer's context and customer data, and test to validate your hypothesis.

Contextualization

Contextualization is about being relevant, making the experience relevant to your customers' intent and their style and channels of communication.

An important part of contextualization is personalization. Personalization covers many tactics. Some marketers think of it as simple tactics like using the customer's name after a log-in. For other marketers it is the creation of extensive personalization using predictive algorithms. When we address personalization in this book, we group it into four categories; all four can work with both known and unknown visitors.

Rules-based personalization	This is the simplest form of personalization and is a proven tactic to optimize conversions. This kind of personalization relies on explicit rules to change content (e.g., when the keyword is "ski holiday," show a ski rental promotion).
	The downside of rules-based personalization is that if you need many rules, it quickly becomes complex and requires a lot of manual maintenance. However, for pages with up to 20 different rules this is still the easiest tactic.
Algorithm personalization	Here we use the power of algorithms, like fuzzy logic or Euclidean distance, to calculate which content is most relevant for visitors based on their In the Moment Behavior.
	Once in place, algorithm personalization is very powerful and is easy to maintain, as it's a matter of profiling content according to a selected taxonomy.
	Algorithms require planning to create a proper taxonomy, profiling content and mapping content to personalized spots. We typically recommend having some experience with personalization before doing this.

Connected personalization	Here personalization is used across different channels, like web, mobile, email, and point of sale. The power of connected personalization is its focus on understanding and connecting the customer's touch points.
	Typically this starts with web and email, as these are the easiest to connect. If you are using a connected platform, this will allow you to recognize a customer coming from email and continue the conversation throughout the web visit. It will also allow you to have triggers on the website where you can respond back through emails.
Automated personalization	This is the most advanced and powerful form of personalization. Machine learning algorithms using a single view of the customer help anticipate the needs of each individual customer. It gives you the power to reach out in the preferred channel at the right time with the right message.

From this stage forward, your marketing will benefit by having as much customer data as possible. A focus on not only collecting, but also connecting the data, will help you to create individual, relevant customer experiences.

In the Optimize stage, you are just getting started with personalization, so rules-based personalization should be your initial focus. Rules-based personalization is simple to get started with and will give you experience in using personalization as well as optimizing outcomes. The work you did in Chapter 6 on the Digital Relevancy Map will help you identify the visitor segments and criteria you need to move forward with rules-based personalization.

If you look at customers, you can determine what is behind their intent, motivations, and preferences by looking at these four areas:

1. In the Moment Behavior

2. Profile data

3. History

4. Connections

In the Moment Behavior

For the majority of visitors through any channel, you will have little or no information. You will have to work with the information you have at the moment. There is no profile data, history, or past connections. In the Moment Behavior is the data you have when the visitor arrives and their behavior is anonymous.

Digital Fingerprint

When visitors arrive at your site, they have what we call the digital fingerprint; in this fingerprint, you get access to a lot of valuable data, data that can help determine the intent of the visitor.

Let's look at some of the data you have access to that could be a predictor of intent.

Marketing campaigns	The campaign visitors respond to tells you something about their intent and stage in the decision journey. Each marketing campaign should have a unique identifier (campaign ID) that can be used to map visitors to the campaign they responded to. By getting the campaign ID, you can identify the intent of the visitor and align the content the visitor sees on the website to the intent of the campaign.
Keywords	Keywords used to be gold mines, as you could use the keywords to classify the stage of a decision journey as well as which product or service the visitor was interested in. However, with Google hiding the organic keywords, using keywords is rarely an option. If you have many visits coming from pay-per-click (PPC) advertising, you still get access to search keywords. This can be used to map visitor intent toward the decision stage and products or services.
Referrals	Referrals are the sites from which the visitor arrives at your site. These could be partners, social sites, search sites, forums, PR links, and so on. Many of these sites could help classify the intent of the visitor, either by mapping referral sites with demographics or by looking at the actual link. The link's wording and context can be used to tell what the visitor expects and therefore the visitor's intent.

Location	Location can refer to country, region, state, city, longitude, and latitude. In many cases this can help map relevant local content to visitors based on their location.
Device	Device gives you information about the device (desktop, mobile, tablet, etc.) used to access your digital channels. This can help you to add context for visitors—for example, presenting quick facts for mobile visitors and additional detail for desktop visitors.
Internet Protocol (IP) Address	Accessing IP addresses can map visitors with known ranges of IP addresses to a specific business, press reporters, competitors, and so on. These can be used to determine the origin of the visitor and, based on that, which content might be relevant for that visitor.

On-Site Behavior

On-site behavior is what the visitor is doing on the site. Visitors are still anonymous, but through their on-site behavior, we are able to detect their intent and use that knowledge to show them relevant content. What follows is a list of what to consider for on-site behavior.

Landing page	The page the visitors arrive at, if different from the home page, then they probably have an interest in the topic of that page. Entering at a deeper page could also imply that they are further along in their decision journey.
Site areas	Many sites have different areas, like Jobs, Services/Products, Thought Leadership, Cases, Training, and so on. Monitoring which areas visitors look at can help classify their intent and interest and can be the foundation for targeting.
Product/service areas	The specific products or services the visitor browses can be used to identify specific items of interest.
Internal search	Looking at which keywords are used to search the site internally will help classify the visitor's interest and intent.
Content type	Looking at the specific pages browsed can help identify a stage in the decision journey. You could map content in different levels between high-level content (home page, About Us, section front pages) and deeper-level content (specific products/services, specifications, price quotes). The deeper the level of content that visitors consume, the further they have progressed in their decision journey.

Situation

The situation could be trending topics that might be top of mind for the person, but it can also include topics such as weather, and time of day. One of our clients found extremely high correlations between specific products being ordered and the dates and weather in specific cities. Using dates and weather, the client could almost exactly predict the volume of visitors from a region.

Profile Data

Profile data is what you already know about the visitor's profile. This can be based on explicit and implicit data.

Profile data can be collected from many sources. Explicit data can be collected from a customer filling in a form with personal information and later be connected to profile data from social networks. The combination enriches the profile with demographic and psychographic data.

Personal Information

Very specific data like name, address, phone, email, company, and so on is typically collected on a form or when somebody opens an account.

Demographics

Gender, age, status, job role, and so on are typically collected through a mix of data coming from forms or provided by connected social networks.

Psychographics

Interests, activities, values, lifestyle, attitudes, and so on can be collected through social networks and on-site behavior. An example could be classifying whether somebody is methodical or spontaneous as part of researching a product or service. This could influence the type of call to action used, something that would be very relevant for the profile.

Preferences

Preferences are more explicit and are based on what we know of the profiles (e.g., which areas the visitors prefer, which content they are looking at, whether they prefer blue over red).

History

History includes all past transactions such as which products or services visitors have bought in the past and their historical activity in the different touch points, like call centers and point of sale. Or if you are a municipality, it could be history of transactions in terms of self-service on the site.

Connections

How is the person connected? You can map the different connections visitors have on social networks. Use this to determine if they are influencers or connectors.

Connect Your Data

The more connected data we have about a visitor or customer, the better and more relevant we can create their experience. If you look at the Customer Life Cycle, you should be able to identify which data are accessed at different stages, as shown in Figure 8.2.

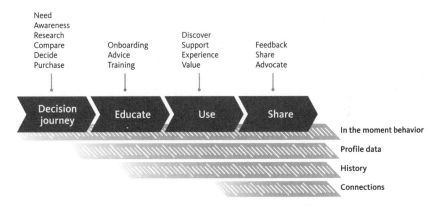

Figure 8.2   Customer Life Cycle with Data Points

In many cases people move through the life cycle in three stages: from unknown to known, from known to customer, and from customer to advocate (see Figure 8.3).

User Scenarios

Once we understand which data we have available, we can look at how visitors and customers use it. Our goal is to get them interested, have them invest more time, and build trust and commitment.

Figure 8.3   Progression from Unknown to Advocate

Personalization is key to making the connection between the visitor's intent and the relevant content. The danger with personalization is that it can easily create very complex scenarios with too many alternative branches. To avoid this we advocate getting started with a few quick wins. Later in this chapter are descriptions of different types of personalization used as quick wins.

The Sitecore® Interest Relevancy Model, shown in Figure 8.4, maps content relevancy (*y*-axis) with visitor interest (*x*-axis); the more relevant, the greater the value (the circle's size shows the value).

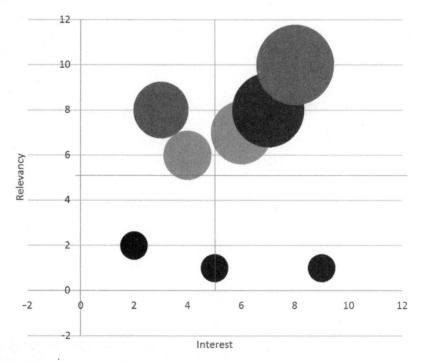

Figure 8.4   Sitecore® Interest Relevancy Model

The model has four quadrants, which can be interpreted like this:

Low Interest, High Relevancy

Here relevant content is used to grab the attention of the visitor. Even though this can be in the early stages of the decision journey and interest in your offerings are low, you want to reduce bounces and engage the visitor to learn more about your offerings.

At this stage most visitors would be unknown and the first important digital goal would be to get simple data, like an email from the visitor.

High Interest, High Relevancy

This is the area of greatest opportunity, as the visitor is engaged and you are able to provide relevant content. You need to leverage this, and at this point you could ask for more commitment, such as more data, or demonstration of advocacy by sharing content with peers.

Low Interest, Low Relevancy

The value from this quadrant is very low, and most likely there will be many visitors bouncing as you are not able to get their attention.

At this point it's very hard to get any commitments in terms of the digital objectives. Focus should be to find and segment those who fall into this quadrant and then use personalization to make their experience more relevant.

High Interest, Low Relevancy

Visitors in this quadrant have high interest, but the site isn't relevant to their interest. This is frustrating for them, as they are interested but don't find what they want.

If you have many visits in this quadrant, your top focus should be using personalization, as this will be a quick win and potentially move them to a higher quadrant. You should also survey users to find why the content or context is not relevant.

Moving from Unknown to Known

Here you are focusing on getting visitors to give information about themselves, most likely personal information, as this will be important in order to recognize them in different channels and send personalized messages. Early stages will limit the amount of information they are ready to give, whereas deeper stages will mean they are more willing to risk giving more information. In both cases, if they feel that what they get in return for providing information is valuable, then they will give you the information.

You can use the Sitecore Interest Relevancy Model (Figure 8.4) to move visitors from unknown to known. For example, assume you are working with an anonymous visitor. You need to look at what data you can get from In the Moment Behavior and use that to contextualize the visitor's experience. Using the Sitecore Interest Relevancy Model, the visitor interest might be low, so the first task is to increase relevancy for the biggest segment of visitors. Once you have found two or three visitor segments that need to be moved in the model, then you can apply personalization to increase their value. You can nurture these same segments to increase their commitment and get more data. You can use this data to personalize more and create a virtuous cycle that builds and builds.

Nissan in Australia began this journey in 2013. The automaker used its website as a key touch point for many potential customers looking to buy a new car. Nissan identified different groups of buyers and their behavior. A key marketing objective was to make the experience more relevant and engage visitors to learn more about the different Nissan car models. Using the intent of visitors, learned from their keyword searches, accessed with In the Moment Behavior, Nissan focused on identifying visitors as early as possible and used that to show relevant content based on the specific models that the visitor searched for. Throughout the visit and subsequent visits, the visitor saw more relevant content about those specific models.

Figure 8.5 shows the default website.

If the visitor enters through a marketing campaign, in this case searching for Nissan Patrol and clicking on the PPC advertising, the home page changes so it's relevant, as shown in Figure 8.6.

Doing this personalization based on the visitor's intent increased the on-site engagement, increased on-site car configurations, and increased the request to test drive Nissan cars.

Moving from Known to Customer

When moving from known to customer, personalization becomes easier. In this situation you already have some information about the visitor—it might just be an email address. The focus is to be relevant

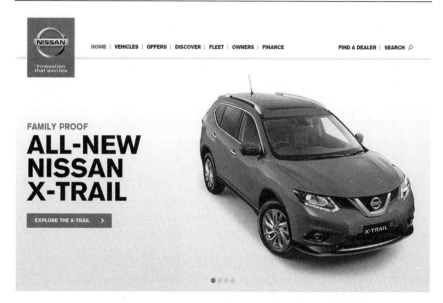

Figure 8.5   Nissan's Default Website

Figure 8.6   Nissan's Website with Personalization

and nurture the visitor along the decision journey until you win that person as a customer.

Unless you are working with e-commerce, the financial conversion of a customer might not happen digitally. The most important objectives could be to continue to get more customer data that can be used to increase relevance and finally convert a sale through the appropriate channel.

In the Moment Behavior and profile data provide insights that can be combined to make the experience more relevant. As you get access to more data, you can use more channels to communicate; for example, an email address will enable you to send relevant email based on the information from In the Moment Behavior.

Monarch Airlines, a leading scheduled leisure airline based in the United Kingdom, strives to be a customer-centric brand, providing superior service at an affordable price. The purpose of its site is to make finding the perfect flight as easily as possible while delivering a great user experience.

Prior to the new customer-focused site, the old site provided a reasonable user experience but didn't push any boundaries in terms of content—it was very much a one-offer-suits-all experience.

With its new site, Monarch has the ability to use various levels of knowledge it has of its individual customers, whether based on the previous site activity of a returning visitor or the digital fingerprint of a new site user, to provide relevancy in what it is showing to them. Through this, Monarch focused on optimizing sales conversions as well as increasing revenue from seat and ancillary sales.

To engage the visitor through a more relevant experience, Monarch has used personalization that includes these insights into visitor intent:

- Flight search
- Booking activity (both incomplete and complete bookings)
- Geolocation
- Keyword search referrer
- Flight search categories

By displaying on the home page near real-time flight prices relevant to personalized promotions, Monarch has increased sales conversions by 5 percent, compared to a 2 percent target.

Moving from Customer to Advocate

Creating customer advocates is an area that many organizations neglect. We need to care for our customers and make sure that they get the most value from using our products and services. We want to create Lifetime Customers. Doing that will increase the number of vocal customers who share their experience with peers. We want our customers to become advocates for us.

There are two main objectives to focus on. The first one is bringing new customers on board while providing them with the best experience. Second, they should be encouraged to share their experience.

An example of this is Auckland Airport. Handling 10 million passengers a year, Auckland Airport's web presence is seen as a critical funnel for engaging airport customers and educating them about the best use of their time and shopping opportunities.

Focusing on educating customers before coming to the airport, Auckland Airport selected parking and getting customers to the most relevant retail stores as its objectives. With recommended in-terminal time reduced by 30 minutes due to increased effectiveness in security, there was less time for passengers to shop in retail stores at the airport. One of the most important objectives was to make the travelers' trips easier and give them more time to shop. This was accomplished by sending visitors information that gave them more time to shop. Visitors booking parking received information relevant to them about their flights and could initiate a series of automated relevant follow-up reminders before coming to the airport. With these messages, Auckland Airport also used the information about the customer to promote relevant retail offers.

Not only did the customer receive better and more relevant messages, but the outcome for Auckland Airport was also significant, with an 84 percent increase in redeemed personalized retail offers compared to nonpersonalized offers.

On its site, Auckland Airport also used In the Moment Behavior to promote relevant messages about the airport as well as retail offers.

This has given invaluable insights into product/brand popularity and leads to a 400 percent increase in traffic to its retail partners. Their bounce rate was reduced by 13 percent.

To work with contextualization, we recommend starting with filling out the Sitecore Digital Relevancy Map described in Chapter 6, which will help map key segments with stages in the decision journey or Customer Life Cycle. The Digital Relevancy Map is critical to informing which content and calls to action are most needed for each visitor segment at each stage in the journey.

As seen in Figure 8.7, personalized content begins with data from In the Moment Behavior and progresses to a combination of In the Moment Behavior, Profile Data, and History. Connections can be used either to build trust or to get commitment to share on social networks.

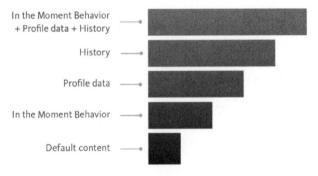

Figure 8.7 Prioritized Levels of Personalization

To help map and prioritize personalization triggers for use with content, we have created the Sitecore® Content Strategy Map (see Figure 8.8), which can be used after filling out the Digital Relevancy Map. It maps spots that should be personalized on the most important pages with specific triggers and content.

The Sitecore® Content Strategy Map can be downloaded at the book's companion website www.ConnectTheExperience.com/SCSM.

	Awareness Stage	
	Which important pages are visited most:	
	Page 1	
	Page 2	
	Which Spot will you use:	
	On Page 1	
	On Page 2	
	What are the triggers and content needed:	
	Trigger A for Spot on Page 1	
	Content needed for Trigger A	
Bob the first-time buyer	Trigger B for Spot on Page 1	
	Content needed for Trigger B	
	Trigger C for Spot on Page 1	
	Content needed for Trigger C	
	Trigger A for Spot on Page 2	
	Content needed for Trigger A	
	Trigger B for Spot on Page 2	
	Content needed for Trigger B	
	Trigger C for Spot on Page 2	
	Content needed for Trigger C	

Figure 8.8 Simplified View of the Sitecore® Content Strategy Map

Testing to Optimize the Experience

For too many years, decisions on which content should be used on different pages, included in email, and highlighted on the home page have been left to chance, to stakeholder opinion, or, even worse, to the sway of shifting politics. Unfortunately, this often results in very poor experiences, where the visitor needs to digest home pages with 40 different calls to action.

Testing doesn't leave things to chance. You can start testing different sets of content and calls to action to learn what works best for your visitors and which have the greatest impact on your objectives.

Improving conversion rates through testing is a well-proven method and is something every organization should do. Testing is easy and can be seen as a low-hanging fruit opportunity to get more conversions. If you don't test, you don't know if your new design, content, video, call to action, or whatever is relevant enough for your visitors to engage with. If you test, you will know exactly which variation on your marketing effort is most relevant for your visitors.

When testing is done by organizations, it's typically limited in scope due to budgets and complexity. Testing needs to be a core of the daily operation and accessible for the entire marketing team instead of limited to small specialist groups.

There are two types of tests that can be used: an A/B split test or a multivariate (MV) test.

A/B Split Test

An A/B split test is a simple test of one element tested against a variation. Elements can be anything from the design of the site to a title, video, picture, or the text on a label within a page.

Multivariate Test

A multivariate (MV) test is a test of several elements with several variations. For example, on a website with landing pages that foster low engagement, multivariate testing allows elements such as headline, picture, and call to action message to be tested against each other to see which combination results in the highest engagement.

Establish a Marketing Taxonomy

As part of the Optimize stage, you should also optimize marketing performance across different channels, both online and offline. Establishing a Marketing Taxonomy will help you identify which channels earn the highest Engagement Value. (Engagement Value is described in Chapter 7, Stage 3—Align.)

A marketing taxonomy identifies channels and subchannels. This same taxonomy code can be used to identify revenue or expenses attributable to a channel and subchannel. Through the use of the taxonomy the channel, revenue, and expenses can be brought together for analysis.

The following table shows part of an online marketing taxonomy. If you have multinational or regional marketing, then you may want to have another level that specifies the country or region.

Taxonomy Code	Channel	Subchannel
PPC Advertising		
41.10.01	PPC advertising	Bing search
41.10.02	PPC advertising	Google search
41.10.03	PPC advertising	LinkedIn search
41.10.04	PPC advertising	YouTube search
41.10.99	PPC advertising	Other search
Display Advertising		
41.11.01	Display advertising	LinkedIn
41.11.02	Display advertising	Facebook
41.11.99	Display advertising	Other display
Social		
41.20.01	Social	Facebook
41.20.02	Social	LinkedIn
41.20.03	Social	YouTube
41.20.04	Social	Twitter
41.20.05	Social	Slideshare
41.20.06	Social	Pinterest
41.20.99	Social	Other
Email Marketing		
41.30.01	Email marketing	Nurture
41.30.02	Email marketing	Purchased list
41.30.03	Email marketing	Customer mailing
41.30.04	Email marketing	Partner mailing
41.30.99	Email marketing	Other

Every marketing campaign will have its own taxonomy code that identifies the campaign's channel and subchannel. For example, a PPC campaign through Google could have a code of 41.10.02 (41 being online, 10 being PPC advertising, and 02 being Google search).

Experience Analytics can use these taxonomy codes associated with each campaign to segment or group marketing efforts and see the Engagement Value or Value per Visit for those channels or campaigns (see Figure 8.9). In Figures 8.9 and 8.10 the taxonomy code appears as a prefix to the channel name.

By segmenting on a specific channel, you get insights about subchannels. In the example shown in Figure 8.10, social has been selected and the subchannels show the value from Twitter, Facebook,

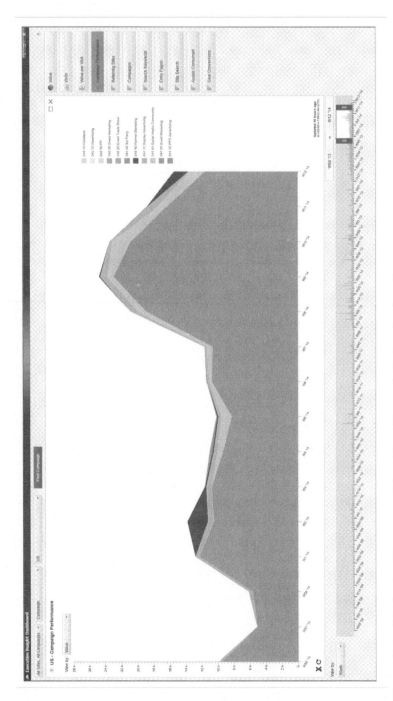

Figure 8.9   Marketing Taxonomy Identifies Channels Being Analyzed

144

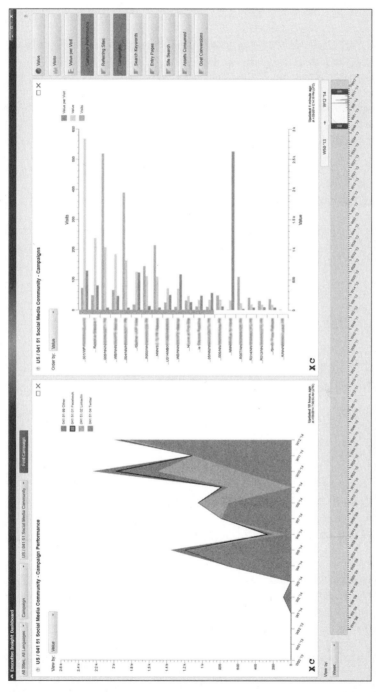

Figure 8.10 Looking at Social Channel Effectiveness

and LinkedIn as well as the value per campaign launched for either of those.

Using a marketing taxonomy makes it easy to compare value and efficiency between channels, even social channels as shown in Figure 8.10.

Using a marketing taxonomy helps get an overview and also allows comparison of performance between channels. Once you have that, you can optimize your cross-channel marketing.

Extend Customer Experiences with New Owned Channels

Another way to optimize the customer experience is to offer customers ways to gain product or service information, while simultaneously engaging with other customers. These customer communities increase the sharing of best practices, knowledge, and increases advocacy.

Collect Data by Applying Content Profiles

Content profiles are similar to taxonomies, but with them you are better able to understand the behavior of each visitor according to the content that visitor consumes.

Think of content profiles as a way for you to identify what visitors are interested in by watching where they go and what they do. Content profiles go beyond the limitation of tags. Content profiles use real-time information from the content consumed by the visitor to create a pattern of information about that visitor. These real-time content profiles can be used to determine the intent and interests of the visitor.

With content profiles, you have the opportunity to create profiles that describe the content on your sites. As visitors move through the website, you can keep track of which content they have touched. When you create the content profiles that describe your content, you must consider what information you want to capture about the visitors.

For example, if you need information about which persona the visitor matches and which services visitors are most interested in, then you will want to create content profiles for personas and services.

If you are a B2B organization with four primary personas, with five different service areas targeting four different industries, then your website's content profile taxonomy could look like this:

Persona Content Profile

- Brad the Business Director

- Dennis the Decision Maker

- Ida the Influencer

- Oliver the Operational

Service Content Profile

- On-site professional services

- Security solutions

- Outsource solutions

- Risk management solutions

- Portfolio solutions

Industry Content Profile

- Manufacturing

- Service

- Government

- Health care

With the content profile taxonomy created, you can apply the profiles to the different content items. A website page or asset can have a combination of different profiles. For example, a page with an industry slant might be 50 percent manufacturing and 50 percent service.

Another example could be applying a downloadable asset titled "Case Study: How We Use Risk Management in Health Care." This asset would have high values in risk management and health

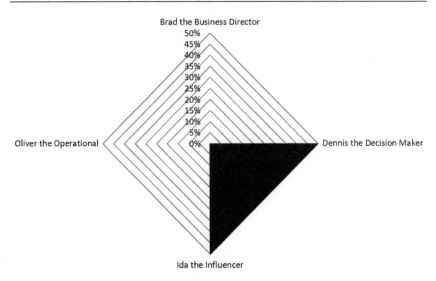

Figure 8.11 Persona Content Profile

care. The personas it was written for could be Dennis the Decision Maker and Ida the Influencer. The content profiles might look like Figures 8.11, 8.12, and 8.13.

As a visitor to the website downloads this document, the content profiles from this asset are added to the visitor's historical data. Over

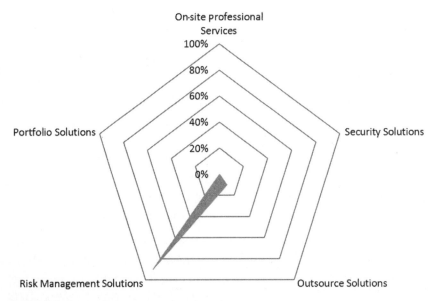

Figure 8.12 Service Content Profile

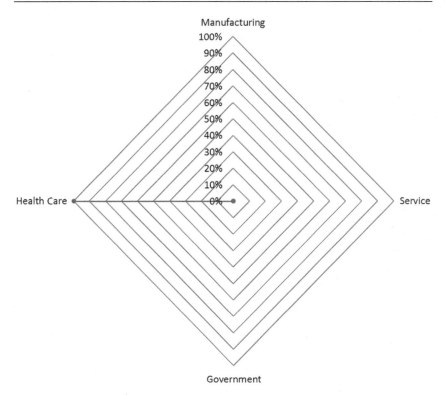

Figure 8.13 Industry Content Profile

time the visitor builds a collection of all the content profiles that person has consumed. The resulting aggregation of data for each visitor gives a clear picture of each visitor's position toward persona, service, and industry.

Based on how the visitor consumes content and using the content profile, we can better understand the visitor. As part of the next stage, Nurture, we also use this insight to apply more advanced personalization, algorithm personalization.

BREAKING BARRIERS

In the Optimize stage, organizations can begin to meet the limits of the systems they are currently using. In this stage the better your connected view of the customer is, the better you can personalize the experience by using data from different marketing systems, social media, email, and so on. This is where you need to begin planning and developing a customer data hub that will give you a single view of the customer.

If your marketing direction has been driven by gut-level artistic feelings, internecine ego-driven opinions, or just random acts of marketing, then you need to get ready to face a major culture change in your marketing organization. The marketing organizations that win now and in the future are data driven. Art and experience are still critical as creative drivers, but it is constant testing that proves what works best. (Imagine the joy of being able to have meetings that aren't hijacked by unfounded opinion. You'll be able to test an idea and prove what works. Just test it and move on.) For a foundation on how to change the culture in your marketing organization, see Chapter 5, Making It Happen!

MOVING TO A HIGHER LEVEL OF MARKETING

While going into the Optimize stage focuses on the low-hanging fruit of optimization, not knowing what to optimize will paralyze you. You need the right approach to enter this stage and succeed. The approach we advocate is to leverage quick wins to build momentum.

The Quick Win Approach

A quick win is a focused effort that builds better experiences in areas where a small change can have a high impact. Using rules-based personalization to increase relevance and A/B testing to improve conversion are excellent tactics for quick wins.

Based on the outcomes, quick wins can be used as business cases to advocate for more initiatives in the Optimize stage—for example, more uses of personalization and testing.

People, Process, and Technology

In the Optimize stage, you can either use external consultants that are experienced in data-driven optimization or use change agents that understand data and the principles of optimization.

People

We do recommend looking for resources that fully understand the nature of data-driven optimization. You may already have a digital analyst that can provide the insights and recommendations for optimization; otherwise it might be time to start looking for additional resources with a strong background in digital analytics and optimization.

Process

To get started with the quick wins, you first need alignment between strategic and marketing objectives. With this you will know what you are optimizing to achieve. Second, you need to complete the Sitecore Digital Relevancy Map. It will help you understand the intent and motives of your different customer groups. Third, analytics will help you find areas for optimization. To execute these improvements, use the Sitecore Content Strategy Map, described earlier in this chapter, to apply optimization.

Technology

To have fully developed customer profiles requires connected data that bring together a single view of the customer, online and offline. This is a key part of the higher levels in the Customer Experience Maturity Model and is described in following chapters.

How Long Will It Take?

Coming from the Align stage, the time to get to Optimize depends on the resources you have available and how connected your technology is. Assuming your data are actionable and available, then focusing on the quick wins could be a matter of weeks for executing and a few more weeks for proving the effects.

The more focused you and your organization are on testing and failing faster, the more agile your approach will be to launching and benefiting from optimization initiatives.

HOW DO YOU KNOW YOU ARE THERE?

You know you are in the Optimize stage when discussion about the customer experience has changed from gut feelings to data-driven. People who have been change agents in the shift to data-driven marketing will start sharing results from optimization. Discussions will focus on phrases like "increases in conversions by using personalization" or "optimizing campaigns with A/B testing." Data-driven marketers will have an important role in influencing which type of content is needed.

All this will lead to different business units using optimization to increase outcomes toward strategic objectives. In return this will foster top management focusing on what marketing can deliver and how marketers play an important part in the strategy. Marketing will move away from "Can we publish this on our site?" to "What is the impact on this objective?" and "How will that affect lead generation?"

It's important to show wins as soon as possible. When doubters see the results of new efforts, they will become believers.

NOTE

1. North American Technographics® Retail Online Benchmark Survey, Q2 2010 (U.S.).

CHAPTER 9

Stage 5—Nurture

The best time to plant a tree was 20 years ago.
The second best time is now.

—Chinese proverb

Organizations in this stage focus on the customer and building strong relationships through automated trigger-based dialogue. Relevant conversations happen in the customer's preferred channels (see Figure 9.1).

THE NURTURE STAGE

If you think about the analogy "crawl, walk, run, fly," the Nurture stage is where you pick up speed and begin to run. Speedy execution is essential. But, when it comes to mastering the Nurture stage, crossing the finish line in a leading position is more about maintaining a steady, high pace as in a marathon running event and less about being the fastest sprinter.

Fundamentally, cross-channel nurturing is the process of systematically inviting conversation, listening, and then engaging with your audience—where and how each customer prefers. If you can generate relevancy for the customer, you may be able to establish a fruitful dialogue.

Listening (listening digitally) is key. Detecting meaningful digital interactions and intent-filled signals enables you to capture data and progressively increase the relevancy of the dialogue. Do this effectively and you earn the trust of your audience. Leveraging this trust in a timely way can enable you to gain commitment—conversions of

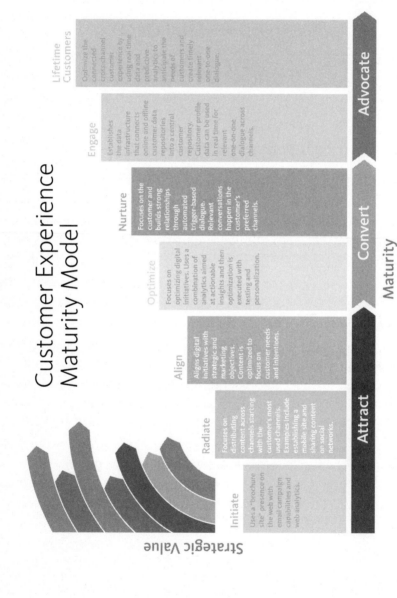

Customer Experience Maturity Model

Strategic Value

Initiate
Uses a "brochure site" presence on the web with email campaign capabilities and web analytics.

Radiate
Focuses on distributing content across channels starting with the customer's most used channels. Examples include establishing a mobile site and sharing content on social networks.

Align
Aligns digital initiatives with strategic and marketing objectives. Content is optimized to focus on customer needs and intentions.

Optimize
Focuses on optimizing digital initiatives. Uses a combination of analytics aimed at actionable insights and then optimization is executed with testing and personalization.

Nurture
Focuses on the customer and builds strong relationships through automated trigger-based dialogue. Relevant conversations happen in the customer's preferred channels.

Engage
Establishes the data infrastructure that connects online and offline customer data into a central customer repository. Customer profile data can be used in real time for relevant one-on-one dialogue across channels.

Lifetime Customers
Optimize the connected cross-channel customer experience by using real-time data and predictive analytics to anticipate the needs of customers and create timely relevant one-to-one dialogue.

Attract   **Convert**   **Advocate**

Maturity

Figure 9.1   Sitecore® Customer Experience Maturity Model™—Nurture Stage

154

valuable digital goals. Technology helps accelerate the nurturing process, but a strategic approach, as spelled out in this chapter, is essential.

Objectives of the Nurture Stage

The main objectives of the Nurture stage are:

- Evolve from multichannel to cross-channel dialogues where focus is customer-centric, digitally listening to behavior and responding in individual customers' preferred channels using, for example, behavioral targeting.

- Make extensive use of automated, personalized email marketing where triggers can be from any online channel and automated email flows include email welcome series, abandoned shopping carts, as well as special purpose automated email flows.

- Incorporate any social channel preferences and capture important behaviors that may take place in preferred social channels so that these behaviors can be leveraged in cross-channel nurturing.

- Monitor key performance indicators (KPIs) in association with stages in the buyer's decision journey.

- Build on your ability to optimize (using personalization and testing as previously covered in the Optimize stage) while fully identifying and leveraging Nurture stage pathways that are made up of the touch points in the channels for which your customers demonstrate a preference.

CASE STORY: QUALITYCARE™ BY LEO PHARMA

How does a pharmaceutical company increase global competitiveness while helping more patients worldwide achieve better treatment outcomes? Acknowledging that there is more to medical care than appointments, drugs, and treatments, LEO Pharma wanted to support their existing portfolio by delivering personalized care and support.

The pharmaceutical industry is experiencing a paradigm shift in which patients increasingly expect to have better and more targeted services and products. Payers expect successful health outcomes and results, and health care professionals want increased quality of life for their patients. Rising to the challenge, LEO Pharma wanted a scalable service that could meet the need for personalized content and patient support.

LEO Pharma develops, manufactures, and markets pharmaceutical drugs to dermatologic and thrombotic patients in more than 100 countries globally. In 2013 LEO Pharma launched the first version of the service—under the brand QualityCare™.

LEO Pharma has amassed valuable knowledge about dermatological conditions and thrombosis through thousands of interviews and extensive research. Provided with the medical expertise and scientific resources, LEO Pharma has been able to identify patient needs and outcomes in order to produce and plan consumer-centric content.

When diagnosed with a chronic disease, patients normally turn to their doctor for information about the disease and treatment options. But the need for support and information is ongoing, and patients may have concerns and questions that arise after visiting the doctor.

Together with its digital agency, LEO Pharma created QualityCare™, a multichannel support service that is designed to engage patients and provide them with tailored and useful information about their treatment, the nature of their condition, and ways to address their concerns during all stages of the disease journey.

On the website, the patient signs up to QualityCare™ by selecting their topics of interest and providing information about their diagnosis and treatment. Once the profile is completed, patients get access to their own personal page with targeted content.

Content is organized according to a unique dialogue plan that triggers various online and offline interventions to empower patients to take control of their disease. The dialogue plan includes interventions in the form of online articles, timely email and text messages, personal nurse calls, and a personalized magazine sent directly to the patient's home address. The dialogue plans are orchestrated using marketing automation, including data-driven print automation to generate the personalized magazine.

The platform makes it possible to track the patient's behavior across channels in order to anticipate potential needs and thereby manage a targeted and personalized dialogue. In this way, user profiling is not only based on the patient's explicitly selected needs (topics of interest), but also on the patient's implicit needs (online actions).

A gradual introduction of content according to the patient's level of engagement and selected topics ensures user commitment throughout the course of the program. Tracking the patient's online behavior can also trigger a call from a nurse, for instance if the patient is looking for information on a particular sensitive topic. During a nurse call, the nurse can support and inform the patient based on predefined nurse scripts, and update the patient's profile with newly discovered information.[1] The dialogue plan including all the content will then adapt accordingly.

QualityCare™ is a master platform with different configuration possibilities. QualityCare™ can be adapted for various disease areas and local markets depending on the market's maturity level, economic standing, and legislation. The first launched solution was targeted patients with psoriasis, followed by two solutions; one targeted actinic keratosis patients and another targeted thrombotic patients.

With QualityCare™, LEO Pharma takes pharmaceutical marketing to the next level by delivering personalized care and support in addition to physical products. Setting new standards for the way pharmaceutical companies can utilize the broad spectrum of digital services to maximize patient outcome, QualityCare™ is a service that adds to and supports LEO Pharma's existing product portfolio.

QualityCare™ is an excellent example of how businesses can combine their unique knowledge with technology-driven personalization to create a fully personalized user experience via the use of multi-channel communication and engagement.

BENEFITS OF NURTURING

A key objective of the Nurture stage is to evolve from the practice of communicating to customers from silos to communicating with connected messages across channels. Customers don't make decisions in straight lines. Instead, decision journeys often follow multiple paths—based on the "scent" of information and individual preferences—that may wind through different digital and nondigital channels. You need to adapt to a connected-customer world where you want to influence the customer decision-making processes when, where, and how it occurs.

You may have a deeper ability in one channel—for example, email—to digitally listen and communicate, but there are limits to how you can use a single channel to build relevancy, trust, and commitment. In the Nurture stage you want to listen and engage where and how the customer prefers. Essentially, you want to evolve from mass marketing to individual relationships. When you are successful, your customers and your organization win.

Benefits to Your Customers

You may think of your customers as multi-channel, but do they see themselves this way? All too often, marketers tend to organize the world around themselves. This marketing-centric viewpoint makes it easier to execute marketing activities, but doesn't match the customer's view of the world. However, effective nurturing requires a customer-centric approach and results in customer-centric benefits.

Customers ultimately want relevant, quality experiences with brands to which they are attracted. If you focus on effectively listening digitally and engaging accordingly in the pathways customers prefer, you stand to generate increased relevancy and engagement. In fact, 82 percent of consumers like reading content from brands when it's relevant.[2] This is an important dynamic you want to leverage when nurturing.

Research shows that consumers have a favorable view about the use of email marketing and website personalization when these capabilities are used in ways that serve their needs.[3] If you can tap into preference, you will be providing better experiences for your customers.

Your ability to listen digitally and engage effectively can serve to build brand recognition and support effects to win brand loyalty. An added positive effect is reducing visitor frustration. Research also shows that 74 percent get frustrated with websites when content, offers, ads, promotions, and the like appear that have nothing to do with their interests.[4] And studies show that about half of the loyalty equation derives from the customer experience during the sales process.[5] A "listening digitally" approach to sales nurturing will pay off in customer loyalty. By keeping the focus on cross-channel communication, your messaging will be unified and more effective.

Benefits to Your Organization

Just as a unified approach to nurturing provides benefits to customers, it also provides important benefits to organizations. By taking steps to engage one-to-one with customers where and how they prefer (while establishing your ability to leverage data), connected nurturing can empower your organization with new capabilities.

One result is better business outcomes. Companies that take a structured approach to marketing activities like nurturing are more likely to improve sales.[6] Other data points support that systematic, relevant communication can reap higher response rates. One such finding shows that new email subscribers are twice as likely to click a link in an email compared to existing subscribers.[7] Nurturing new subscribers is an example presented later in this chapter.

Greater cross-organizational efficiencies are another benefit. Studies show that marketing organizations that collaborate are more efficient and effective.[8] By establishing measurable, reusable nurturing processes that are designed and implemented across channels, marketing organizations should be able to improve collaboration and break down silos.

Organizations that strategically focus on cross-channel nurturing tend to develop more productive sales and marketing processes. This sharper focus can lead to higher productivity and improved business results. For example, a B2B software company that established new processes (in an effort to more tightly interlock sales and marketing) implemented marketing automation processes to almost double its opportunities and increase revenue from new sales agreements by 178 percent.[9]

And then there are competitive advantages. Companies that use three or more of the types of nurturing methods described in this book—for example, personalization, testing, and marketing automation—saw a large increase in sales conversion rates.[10] A by-product of this agility is higher-quality marketing initiatives— unified marketing initiatives. Such initiatives improve synergies across different parts of the organization to achieve more of a combined effect.

WHAT YOU NEED TO DO TO NURTURE CUSTOMERS

Someone once said, "One machine can do the work of 50 ordinary men." A similar analogy can be made about nurture marketing. You are in effect building a machine—your marketing machine. But what are the key ingredients that will, one hopes, enable you to make a measurable contribution to sales while optimizing the marketing spend?

How to Approach Nurturing

Step 1 is to develop an approach that works. Like the other levels in the Customer Experience Maturity Model, you need to step back and identify the people, processes, and technology that are needed in light of your strategic business objectives and strategic marketing objectives. An important question to ask when developing an approach to nurturing is: How fast do you want to run? It is essential that you also consider how fast you are able to run given the types of constraints your organization, like many, may face. These constraints are likely to include budget limitations, connected technology, lack of process, competencies gaps, and so on.

For most organizations the best approach is often a phased approach. Although it is easy to get excited about the sheer capabilities of various nurture marketing tool sets, several customer cases show that companies that have taken a phased approach can achieve successful business outcomes while building the experience that has helped them to continuously improve.[11]

When mapping out a phased approach, be sure that each phase contains nurturing experiments—especially early phases. Experimenting and understanding what fails and what succeeds makes up a proven approach to learning faster. Nissan Australia experimented with cross-channel nurturing that used website personalization. The experiments involved different placements of personalized content. Nissan found that placing a personalized offer on the home page in place of the hero carousel was more effective than using personalization in a deep link to a product page.[12]

Timeliness is essential for nurturing. Therefore, a key mechanism for nurturing is automation. Deciding what to automate is consequently one of the most important decisions when defining your approach to nurturing. A number of specific recommendations are provided later in this chapter, but in general consider combining capabilities and thinking in terms of visitor journeys. For example, consider combining capabilities like personalization, behavior-based profiling, and email automation while segmenting for device.

This may sound complex, but in a phased approach you can start simply and work toward leveraging the capabilities that make the best sense given your specific objectives and target segments. You want to lay the right foundation when defining your approach so that you have the most powerful capabilities—for use in combination—when needed.

In effect, when establishing your approach, you want to be agile and accurate. Just as a military commander strives to "shoot, move, and communicate" at the same time, the approach you define to nurturing should put your organization in a position to execute—at a high pace—nurturing programs that create quality customer experiences.

Identify Processes to Nurture Customers

In a nutshell, nurturing is listening and subsequently communicating relevantly in order to build trust and ultimately gain commitment. You listen digitally at scale using technology and detect preferences (for example, does a given customer prefer to communicate in a social channel?); meaningful interactions (for example, micro goal conversions); and meaningful signals (for example, is a given prospect asking for purchasing advice?).

Based on what you (or your nurturing tool) hear, the relevancy in your communication is ideally achieved using targeted messaging (perhaps based on collected data and personalization) and timeliness that takes place in the channel that a given customer prefers. Think of this capability as progressive targeting.

Starting with the first digital "touch" when a potential customer first visits your website, you want to be able to use data to increase relevancy. As the touches (visits) from this individual customer occur and progress, you want to progressively leverage profile data that is collected as well as in-the-moment actions and behavior. The result should hopefully be a connected conversation composed of multiple touch points. Consider progressive targeting when designing nurture processes (see Figure 9.2).

When determining what to nurture, you may find there are two types of candidates: the obvious and the not so obvious. Let's start with the obvious candidates. What are some of the touch points that you have in place today, and how could they be used for nurturing? Here are some suggestions:

- *Email welcome series*. Research shows that new email subscribers are twice as likely to click a link in a received email compared to existing subscribers.[13] Consider establishing a series of emails that are automatically triggered, over time, to new email subscribers. Consider ways to humanize the sender, subject line, and body of these emails. A key objective of the welcome emails is to build trust. Avoid strong calls to action until recipients demonstrate (via interactions with micro goals) that you have earned trust.

- *Email countdown series*. An event such as a subscription renewal or life cycle milestone could warrant a series of emails that leverage the relevancy of the event or milestone. For example, include a series of emails prior to the renewal date for an insurance policy, club membership, or software subscription.

- *Win-back email series*. Triggered emails that contain relevant content have been shown to generate substantial conversion rates. Recognizable, meaningful content is a key ingredient, as is timeliness. For example, one e-commerce study showed that while 72 percent of site visitors who place items into an online shopping cart do not complete the purchase, a sequence of triggered emails containing relevant content will recover between 10 percent and 30 percent of the buyers.[14]

With email nurturing, keep in mind that supporting the customers' preferred device or devices is a key aspect of being relevant. Emails that do not render fast enough on a smartphone, for example, lead to fewer opens and clicks compared to emails that are optimized. A study among smartphone and tablet users found that

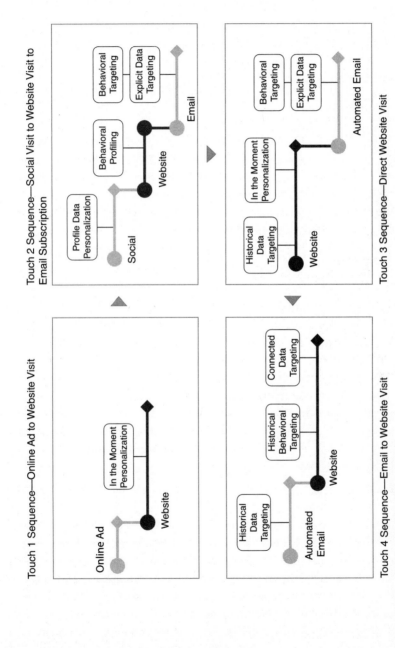

Figure 9.2 Progressive Nurturing

59 percent of participants said download speed was the leading factor for determining whether a mobile website was "good."[15]

What about the less obvious candidates for nurturing? What are some of the scenarios you could consider that you may not have in place today?

- *Dynamic email welcome series.* Research shows that a basic email welcome series can generate above-average open and click-through rates.[16] Taking the concept a step further, the website visits produced by these emails are excellent candidates for nurturing. For example, an email welcome nurturing sequence could be extended to detect important micro goal conversions during website visits. The nurturing process could, for example, spawn more relevant and timely emails based on behavior and interactions during the email series process (as illustrated in Figure 9.3).

- *Attribution nurturing.* The "attractor factor" that generated a first website visit can be used for segmentation or personalization. For example, the attractor factor for a first visit may have been an online ad. Visitors who are attracted by an ad could be added to a nurture flow based on that ad's topic. The flow can update selected visitors into new segments as subsequent visits occur and visitors perform (or do not perform) certain interactions. A first-time visitor who was attracted by an online ad or a social post can be added to a segment as an anonymous prospect. If the visitor, on a subsequent visit, subscribes to email or signs up for a seminar, then additional personalized messages can leverage that email or seminar the visitor was interested in.

- *Behavior-based nurturing across channels.* Studies in the area of stated preferences versus revealed preferences show that people don't always actually do what they say they will do. When you want to tap into in-the-moment preferences for use in marketing, a connected customer experience platform gives you the best of both worlds: you can ask for and capture explicit preferences, and you can track and store behaviors that indicate revealed preferences. Consider using website visitor profiling for nurturing in social channels. For example, assume a logged-in visitor who previously submitted an

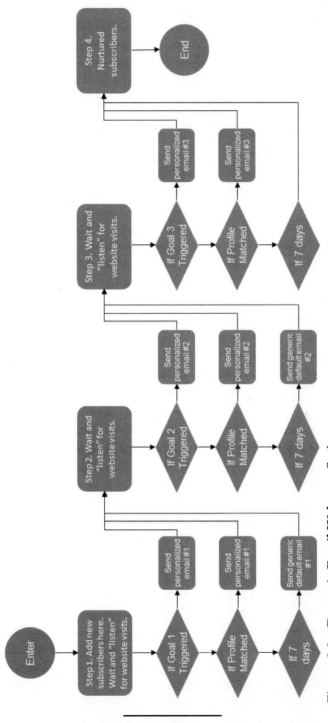

Figure 9.3 Dynamic Email Welcome Series

explicit preference for the mid-priced product visits and demonstrates implicit interest in the high-priced product. Using in-the-moment behavior matching as a trigger, the visitor could be added to a high-priced segment. The segment could be used for personalizing website content or personalized social posts, email content, and sales follow-up.

- *Nurture using triangulation.* Websites have the ability to identify a variety of behaviors in real time. Consider capturing different types of distinct behaviors and using them to triangulate the visitor's behavior into a narrow segment. For example, assume you have three different content profiles you want to track: one for personas (identifying personal characteristics), one for product category preference, and one for buying phase. Consider what you can deduce if a visitor looking at new cars views inexpensive car models, then checks sporty cars, and finally uses an online calculator to calculate product financing. You could use those three content profiles to personalize the visitor's current visit and future visits as a qualified potential buyer of low-cost sporty models. If you also tracked that unique visitor's preferred channels, then you could send or display very relevant messages, perhaps telling of a dealer in the area with a forthcoming sale on a model fitting this visitor's interest.

- *Nurturing using targeted app messages.* In cases where email is less effective or not a preferred channel, nurture messaging to apps installed on smartphones is proving a viable alternative. In China, for example, where consumer email marketing has a limited effect due to the widespread practice of selling email lists, banks have begun to embrace apps, such as WeChat, to send consumer-oriented messages to banking customers. In Russia, Facebook messaging is used among businesses for similar reasons. Wireless beacon technologies—that have the potential to send coupons to apps on the smartphones of in-store shoppers—offer interesting nurturing possibilities.

- *Nurturing for customer activation, retention, and reselling.* With customers' increased use of digital channels throughout the entire Customer Life Cycle, companies are increasingly looking at ways to use digital channels to support key business objectives. Nurturing can play a key role here.

For example, data from a customer relationship management (CRM) or customer transaction system can feed into a customer experience platform to add customers to a nurturing program.

When considering your nurturing processes, focus on how and where your customers prefer to communicate. Consider that your objective is to nurture micro goals and build trust to ultimately gain macro conversions. The journey is part of the reward.

BREAKING BARRIERS

What are some of the common barriers to establishing an effective cross-channel nurturing capability? From a tools and technology perspective, you may think the barriers are low. After all, the marketing automation market is growing by about 50 percent annually. Although this may be the case, 85 percent of B2B marketers using marketing automation platforms feel they are not using their systems to their full potential.[17] Do common barriers play a role here?

You may find that a lack of strategic commitment is a barrier to establishing your ability to master the Nurture stage. If organizations are not prepared to prioritize nurturing in terms of executive commitment, budget, training, and strategic marketing methodology—these organizations may fall short. Shortsightedness, organizational silos, and lack of budget follow-through have been shown to be reasons for failures in marketing automation programs.

Effective cross-channel nurturing requires much more than technology. One example is content. Ongoing nurturing requires effective content. Such content may be in the form of rich media, new creative ideas, and thoughtful leadership editorial material. If there is no structure in place to supply these ingredients, the nurture machine may grind to a stop.

Lack of process and an inability to target customers are additional barriers. With regard to process, the ability to leverage a connected customer experience platform successfully requires diligent project management. If this is not part of the culture of a marketing organization, beware. Practices such as project planning, accountability, process documentation, and marketing taxonomy are essential.

The same goes for an inability to target. An inability to define customer personas greatly limits nurturing effectiveness. In a Marketing Sherpa benchmark report about marketing barriers, marketers indicated that their insufficient insight into target audiences and lack of a clear value proposition—key elements to effective nurturing—were top barriers to marketing success.[18]

An additional barrier may be your current technology. You may face technology barriers that inhibit your ability to listen digitally and execute across channels and in the channels where given customers prefer to communicate.

Overcoming barriers such as these may not be easy. In the following section you find strategic and specific actions you can take to break down barriers and master the Nurture stage.

MOVING TO A HIGHER LEVEL

What is required to master the Nurture stage? How long will it take? Where are investments needed, and what types of competencies and skills are needed? Assuming you are in control of the previous stages in the maturity model, here are key considerations for mastering the Nurture stage.

Steps for Developing an Approach to Cross-Channel Nurturing

You should establish a foundation on which to grow your nurturing ability. Many of the following steps will have been partially or completely finished as you worked through the previous stages. Important steps for developing nurturing in your organization include:

- Starting with your strategic business objectives and high-priority marketing objectives, identify the micro and macro goals you will use to achieve these objectives.

- Identify the broad segments and subsegments of prospects and customers that you want to attract and who are attracted to your goals.

- Begin developing a single view of the customer by establishing a connected customer profile. The profile should be designed to scale as well as to contain a variety of data—contact information, channel preferences, device preferences, persona, profiles behavior, campaign history, responses, transactions, and so on.

- Be prepared to experiment. A key objective with the Nurture stage is to master the ability to engage across channels. It will invariably require research as well as trial and error to identify the combinations of segments, channels, goals, and persuasive content to develop winning formulas.

- In developing your approach to nurturing, identify the mistakes you want to avoid. This could be an important step toward actually avoiding mistakes and pitfalls.

- Ensure you have commitment from executives. Consider conducting the quick wins process (described and linked to in Chapter 13) to arm yourself with the ammunition to reinforce your business case.

- Create a strategy document. Take a quality-in, quality-out approach where you commit yourself to milestones and periodic reviews.

Identifying Nurture Processes

What should your nurture processes be? The answer is part art and part science. First off, identify the channels your customers prefer. You want to meet your customers where they prefer and not where it is primarily convenient for you to execute as a marketing organization.

If you do not have firsthand knowledge of your customers' preferred channels, conduct research to identify the channels that your type of customer prefers. Also, understand the channel preferences of your competitors. Research may help here as well.

Some of the nurture processes you identify may include traditional channels, but consider experimenting in nontraditional channels to understand preferred channels as mapped to different customer segments.

Identify types of content that are persuasive for the different segments you are targeting in the different buyer journey phases.

Don't think in terms of individual pieces of content. Think in terms of customer dialogues where you want content to support the process of driving attraction, trust, and commitment. Identify the key interactions and calls to action that are effective for different segments in their preferred channels.

Leverage proven processes. Examine existing interactions and current calls to action, and consider ways to create automated dialogues that start or lead up to these calls to action. Typical examples include sign-up forms, social shares, requests for contact, and transaction completions. If a process—for example, an online ad that drives conversions—is currently effective, you should be able to increase the effectiveness of the process using structured nurturing.

Identifying Technology Needs

Depending on your approach and processes, the technology you use can vary. Here are guidelines, based on capabilities that you can use to identify technology for cross-channel nurturing.

- *Automation*. The automation capability for the Nurture stage should give you the ability to reach across channels. The tool should let you listen in one channel and, based on interactions and signals in that channel, execute in a different channel. It is paramount that this cross-channel tracking capability be website-centric. Given that high business–value interactions and calls to action take place on your website, you must have the ability to use automation on the website to nurture the pathways leading to the conversion points.

- *Multivariate testing*. In the Optimize stage, you performed A/B split tests. In the Nurture stage, the technology you use must enable you to perform multivariate tests. When it comes to multivariate testing and nurturing, it is essential that you are able to conduct experiments to test hypotheses regarding nurture pathways, visitor segments, sources of attribution, and the like.

- *Personalization*. The personalization capability you established in the Optimize stage should be extended in the Nurture stage. To generate increasingly relevant one-to-one dialogues, you need technology that enables you to present personalized content (in the preferred channel and adapted for the preferred device) based on all forms of personalization. This includes algorithm-based personalization. And you need to be able to measure the effects. An important consideration here is the ability to centrally store visitor profiles and significant behavioral choices for use in further generating relevancy.

- *Campaign attribution.* Understanding the campaigns that attract visitors to nurture pathways as well as campaigns that feed conversions is essential. The technology should enable you to attribute campaigns and to use campaign attributions when generating relevancy along nurture pathways.

- *Integrated e-commerce.* In scenarios where e-commerce is used, the technology should enable you to employ nurturing capabilities in the shopping catalog as well as in the checkout processes.

- *Customer tracking.* The ability to track customers from anonymous to known to logged in is an important technological capability for nurturing. This tracking uses techniques like resolving IP numbers into business names. While this has been important in business-to-business (B2B) settings, the capability is also applicable in business-to-consumer (B2C) settings. Although customer tracking is used in a basic way in the Optimize stage, in the Nurture stage the technology should permit you to store customer tracking information centrally in preparation for the connected customer profile.

- *Deeper social integration.* The technology should enable you to evolve from simply listening to social channels to also engaging in social channels. The ability to post personalized content in social channels (as well as simultaneously in other channels) is essential. It should also be possible to collect data, such as profile data, and feed this to the connected customer profile.

- *Content distribution.* The technology should support cross-channel dialogues. Capabilities such as tag injection into foreign systems (for example, HTML pages) is one example of how content distribution can be accomplished. Content distribution should also be supported for retargeting, communities, devices, information kiosks, smartphone and tablet apps, print, and so on.

Email Marketing

The email technology used for cross-channel nurturing should ideally be coupled with the automation technology and website. If these capabilities coexist in the same system, the tracking, reporting, and analytics intelligence is greater. To truly measure and optimize nurture pathways, the email capability should track the journeys of email recipients who click through email links, visit channels (most importantly the website), and convert goals. The more closely coupled the email tracking is to website tracking, the easier it is to nurture email visits and measure the nurturing performance for email visitors. In addition, ease of execution is essential. But trading off cross-channel tracking capabilities for ease of execution will limit possibilities to nurture visitor pathways effectively. As the maturity stages increase, so does the need for specialized competencies. Cross-channel, data-driven nurturing is a step up in complexity—and business value—compared to traditional email marketing and silo-based email automation.

If the top priority is to make nurturing easy for marketers to execute, this may be a setup for failure. The payoff with the Nurture stage is developing a capability to listen in the channels where your customers are and use the signals to generate conversions on your website. Accomplishing this requires specialized competencies and skills. Find an effective balance between ease of execution and effort of execution. Some of the skills and roles needed include customer acquisition marketers, channel experts, content marketers, and expert tools users.

Effective cross-channel nurturing requires diligent project management. Not only can the project management role help to drive projects to completion, but this function can also help to manage project costs. Project management should be used on an ongoing basis to manage the continuous digital optimization activities that we recommend. Calculating return on investment for cross-channel nurture initiatives could be a responsibility of the project manager.

How Long Will It Take?

How long will it take to reap the rewards of an effective cross-channel nurture machine? Although the answer will vary from one organization to the next, a phased approach is recommended. Phase one could be developing an approach. With steps such as developing a proposal (including analysis and strategy) and securing executive buy-in, the time estimate for phase one could reasonably be three to six months. Phase two could be a limited implementation and require another three to six months. This is a critical phase and may include activities such as establishing a project plan for pilot evaluation, building and testing the implementation, and conducting optimization trials. Thereafter additional phases for rolling out the solution would depend on factors such as business priorities and geographical strategies.

How Do You Know You Are There?

You know you're in control of the Nurture stage when you can personalize journeys that cross multiple channels. These journeys should culminate at personalized content and goals on your website.

When analyzing your recent website traffic, you should segment traffic by channel, and be able to see that specific website-based personalization variants contribute to micro and macro goal conversions (and Engagement Value). Importantly, the specific personalization variants should contain content, data, or signals that originate from the segmented channel. For example, for a website marketing automobiles, visitors who were attracted by online ads about eco-friendly family cars should ideally respond to personalization variants about eco-friendly family themes.

When analyzing recently acquired leads and customers, you should have basic stored data that shows preferred channels as well as perhaps first and last campaign attributions. When analyzing conversions, you should ideally see that personalization variants (deployed on the website or deployed to the attributing channel) have contributed to micro goal conversions (in addition to macro conversions).

Finally, when assessing brand perception and customer feedback, you should receive indications that the degree of relevancy in your communication is above average for your industry and is a contributing factor to positive brand recognition and feedback.

As mentioned at the outset of this chapter, mastering the Nurture stage is not unlike competing in a marathon running event. Only in this case, the running never stops. And just like a marathon, winning requires preparation, nonstop execution, and enormous determination.

NOTES

1. Geoffrey E. Bock, "LEO Pharma Personalizes Consumer Health Information with QualityCare™," Bock & Company, January 2014, www.sitecore.net/customers/selected-customers/healthcare/leopharma.aspx.

2. "The Content Marketing Revolution," Content Marketing Association, www.the-cma.com/uploads/documents/cma-01.jpg.

3. "The Marketer's Playbook: Aligning Marketing Strategies with Consumer Expectations," [x+1], 2013, www.xplusone.net.

4. "Online Consumers Fed Up with Irrelevant Content on Favorite Websites, According to Janrain Study," July 31, 2013, http://janrain.com/about/newsroom/press-releases/online-consumers-fed-up-with-irrelevant-content-on-favorite-websites-according-to-janrain-study/.

5. Matthew Dixon and Brent Adamson, "The One Kind of Sales Rep Who Does Best at B2B," *Forbes*, February 3, 2012, www.forbes.com/sites/forbesleadershipforum/2012/02/03/the-one-kind-of-sales-rep-who-does-best-at-b2b/, and www.executiveboard.com/exbd/sales-service/challenger/b2b-loyalty-drivers/index.page.

6. "Econsultancy Conversion Rate Optimization Report 2013," Econsultancy.com Ltd, October 2013.

7. Jeanne Jennings, "The Honeymoon Effect," ClickZ, April 2, 2012, www.clickz.com/clickz/column/2143623/honeymoon-effect.

8. "How IT Enables Productivity Growth," McKinsey Global Institute, November 2002; Tammy Erickson, "Collaboration Will Drive the Next Wave of Productivity Gains," *Harvard Business Review*, May 2, 2012, http://blogs.hbr.org/2012/05/collaboration-will-drive-the-n/.

9. David Kirkpatrick, "Marketing Automation Case Study: One Marketer's 5 Step Process from Vendor Selection to a 178% Increase in Deals," Marketing Sherpa, November 23, 2011, www.marketingsherpa.com/article/case-study/one-marketers-5-step-process.

10. "Econsultancy Conversion Rate Optimization Report 2013," Econsultancy.com Ltd, October 2013.

11. "Optimizing the Nissan Australia Online Experience," July 2013, www.sitecore.net/Resources/Confirm.aspx?id=7daea472-98c8-480a-b605-675c741bb3cd.

12. Ibid.

13. Jennings, "Honeymoon Effect."

14. "11th Annual Merchant Survey: Customer Experience Escalation: Making the Right Choices in a Connected World," April 17, 2012, www.e-tailing.com/content/?p=2849.

15. "Digital Design Shift: From Mobile to Multichannel," 2013 Sitecore Whitepaper, study conducted by Millward Brown and Dynamic Logic, http://www.sitecore.net/Learn/Resources-Library/White-Papers/Digital -Design-Shift-From-Mobile-to-Multichannel.aspx

16. Adam T. Sutton, "Post-Sale Nurturing: Nonprofit's Email Welcome Series Beats Newsletter Open Rate 47%, Marketing Emails 257%," Marketing Sherpa, February 7, 2012, www.marketingsherpa.com/ article/case-study/nonprofits-email-welcome-series-beats.

17. Matt Senatore, "Eight is NOT Enough: Increasing Adoption of Market-ing Automation Platforms," www.siriusdecisions.com/blog/eight-is-not-enough-increasing-adoption-of-marketing-automation-platforms/.

18. Marketing Sherpa, 2012 B2B Marketing Benchmark report.

CHAPTER 10

Stage 6—Engage

Do what you do so well that they will want to see it again and bring their friends.

—Walt Disney

O rganizations in this stage establish a data infrastructure that con- nects online and offline customer data repositories into a central customer repository. Customer profile data can be used in real time for relevant one-on-one dialogue across channels (see Figure 10.1).

THE ENGAGE STAGE

In your quest to move up the Customer Experience Maturity Model, consider the Engage stage as an important staging ground. It is here where you want to fully establish your infrastructure to connect data, build a complete connected view of the customer, and leverage data in real time. Your ability to collect, connect, and act immediately on data will give you the potential to grow your business and differentiate your value proposition toward customers and competitors.

In the era we live in, customer expectations are changing rapidly. The convenience that digital channels afford customers in decision journeys fuels expectations for positive experiences. The demand for customer relevancy has never been greater. This demand, in turn, now drives the imperative for companies to attain the single view of the customer.

Mastering the Engage stage may require a transformation of your business. Your efforts to start designing customer experiences that cross channels will drive this transformation. In the Engage stage you want

Customer Experience Maturity Model

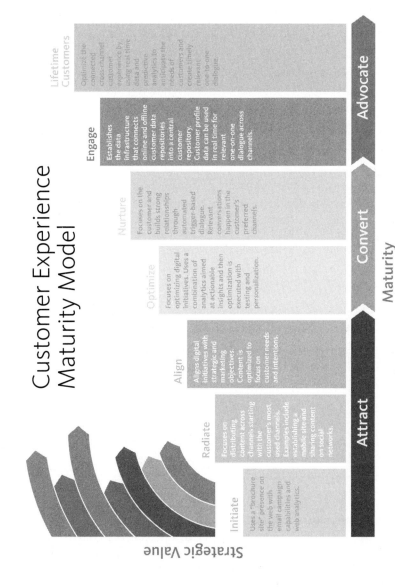

Initiate
Uses a "brochure site" presence on the web with email campaign capabilities and web analytics.

Radiate
Focuses on distributing content across channels starting with the customer's most used channels. Examples include establishing a mobile site and sharing content on social networks.

Align
Aligns digital initiatives with strategic and marketing objectives. Content is optimized to focus on customer needs and intentions.

Optimize
Focuses on optimizing digital initiatives. Uses a combination of analytics aimed at actionable insights and then optimization is executed with testing and personalization.

Nurture
Focuses on the customer and builds strong relationships through automated trigger-based dialogue. Relevant conversations happen in the customer's preferred channels.

Engage
Establishes the data infrastructure that connects online and offline customer data repositories into a central customer repository. Customer profile data can be used in real time for relevant one-on-one dialogue across channels.

Lifetime Customers
Optimize the connected cross-channel customer experience by using real-time data and predictive analytics to anticipate the needs of customers and create timely relevant one-to-one dialogue.

Strategic Value

Attract   Convert   Advocate

Maturity

Figure 10.1   Sitecore® Customer Experience Maturity Model™—Engage Stage

to magnify and strengthen the ability to increase relevancy that you have mastered in the previous maturity levels. And you want to lay the groundwork for the next level where you will harness this cross-channel data to predict the needs of your customers.

To accomplish this effectively and efficiently, marketers must have a single, connected view of the customer as a starting point. The ability to leverage the connected view—in real time—is essential. A single view of the customer is not about knowing everything there is to know about each customer. It's more about smart data than big data. It's about knowing what is meaningful to a given customer—at a time when it is useful—and acting accordingly.

Get this right and not only will you provide meaningfully relevant experiences for your customers, but you will also increase your ability to achieve your business objectives efficiently. As described in this chapter, mastering the Engage stage will heighten your ability to evolve from *talking at* mass audiences to *conversing with* individual human beings.

Objectives of the Engage Stage

The main objectives of the Engage stage are:

- Integrate and bridge the online and offline worlds by establishing one shared view of the customer in a central customer data hub. The hub should be universally accessible (for example, in the cloud) and have the technological capabilities to respond to high volumes of requests in real time.

- Establish the technology infrastructure and governance needed to grow and leverage a connected customer profile in a marketing data hub that connects data that might otherwise reside in disconnected database silos.

- Enhance data in the marketing data hub by capturing and storing customer attributions, channel preferences, cross-channel behaviors, traversed pathways, implicit behavioral data, and explicit data.

- Orchestrate large-scale and small-scale marketing initiatives that combine capabilities mastered in earlier customer experience stages such as simple personalization, algorithm personalization, connected personalization, testing, and marketing automation to leverage the single view of the customer in the marketing data hub.

- Leverage online and offline marketing automation such as printing of a personalized brochure based on online browsing behavior.

- Focus on generating advocacy among customers, and reward your vocal advocates who attract new customers.

Case Story: AustralianSuper

How do you deliver improved customer experiences when your members tend to be infrequent visitors to your website? The answer for leading Australian retirement savings fund, AustralianSuper, was to connect data repositories and leverage systemic, data-driven personalization in its digital marketing.

With this, AustralianSuper members benefit from highly relevant self-service experiences that have resulted in a dramatic increase in engagement and usage.

Serving more than 2.1 million members and 200,000 employers, and managing over AUD $75 billion in members' assets, AustralianSuper has a clear mission: to give its members their best possible retirement. Australia boasts the world's third largest retirement or superannuation asset pool, with about AUD $1.8 trillion in assets. The Australian public's awareness and interest in superannuation have risen steadily.

In 2010, AustralianSuper recognized a need to provide simplified and more tailored experiences for its members. But due to the nature of retirement savings, where retirement funds are deposited automatically, the number of members logging in regularly was not high.

At the time, its members were required to log in to different systems to access different types of information, including a member's superannuation account and, optionally, account information about life insurance and income protection insurance. Paper-based information was not uncommon. As AustralianSuper explained, it was a "vanilla" experience and usage was low—only about 15 percent of transactions were completed online.

AustralianSuper continuously looks for ways to leverage its scale and serve its members more efficiently and with higher levels of engagement. With changing expectations among its members, Australian-Super saw an opportunity to simplify the member experience while enabling them to take greater control through more personalized and informed self-service actions.

The strategy included unification of systems and providing a highly secure single sign-on capability. An important step was to connect data—member data, online forms, booking systems, syndicated content feeds, insurance underwriting applications, and web content. The personalization engine was extended to combine a member's browsing activity with his or her detailed profile.

To help members achieve better outcomes, AustralianSuper developed a personalization strategy based on the connected data. The objective was to match each logged-in member with relevant online tools—such as informative videos for making extra contributions, calculators for contributions, and publications for investor education—based on available personal data.

A member segmentation matrix was developed and 12 data-driven profiles and six behavioral profiles were created. As visits occur, these profiles are used in combination with specially developed algorithms. The combination of real-time profiling and the algorithms enables the system to serve the most relevant online tools, calls to action, and content to the logged-in member. Personalized experiences were enabled for both logged-in and anonymous visitors.

This increased relevance has resulted in significant increases in engagement, usage, and completed self-service transactions. Compared to benchmarks established prior to deploying the new solution, AustralianSuper was able to achieve:

- A 250 percent increase in self-service transactions as a percentage of all fund enquiries and transactions

- A 40 percent increase in members joining AustralianSuper online (excluding deemed members)

- Doubling of monthly traffic and tripling of monthly member logins

- A 230 percent increase in annual visits

This part of the journey for AustralianSuper was not without its challenges—both technical and organizational—however, the results have been very encouraging and provide a solid base for the next phase. This is a good example of how organizations can take steps toward creating a more unified and personalized view to the customer.

BENEFITS OF ENGAGE: THE SINGLE VIEW OF THE CUSTOMER

While research shows that only a minority of companies use data to form a single view of the customer (just 30 percent of companies according to our study highlighted in Chapter 4), consumers reward companies that do and punish those that don't.[1] When asked, 84 percent of consumers said they would walk away from a company that, in effect, did not listen to their data, whereas more than half of these same consumers would "actively recommend and endorse a company that effectively managed and linked its customer data to inform marketing campaigns."[2] What's more, certain types of companies, retailers, for example, indicate that one of their top barriers to creating consistent customer experiences and leveraging multichannel opportunities is the lack of a single view of the customer.[3]

Benefits to Your Customers

When companies establish and use a single view of the customer, how do customers benefit in practice? Benefits to customers include:

- *Richer outcomes*. Based on the intelligence provided via the connected customer profile, customers can achieve more rewarding outcomes when interacting with brands. Outcomes may include optimal buying decisions, more efficient self-service, and perfectly timed access to information—for example, purchasing last-minute business-travel flight tickets on a high-demand route or the ability for a consumer to schedule with one click on a mobile app a test drive at the nearest dealership. According to research, almost half (43 percent) of consumers would "make additional purchases or return to an organization that had correctly marketed products to them based on their personal situation."[4]

- *More control.* As the demand for convenience becomes an increasingly important brand differentiator, data-driven intelligence can be used to provide new levels of customer convenience. For example, when making restaurant reservations, preferences based on previous visits as well as explicit data can be used for preferred table selection.

- *Reduced waste.* As the use of digital channels increases in the decision journey, so, too, does the possibility of consumers wasting time due to increasing amounts of irrelevant online advertising and broadly targeted email marketing. However, a side effect of contextualized experiences is increased productivity and reduced waste of time and energy. For example, an office manager in charge of buying office supplies can receive personalized email promoting regularly purchased products that are synchronized with a demonstrated reordering pattern.

Benefits to Your Organization

Just as the single customer view generates benefits for customers, the capability also provides benefits for organizations. Leveraging data with a single view of the customer helps companies execute sales and marketing activities that lead to outcomes such as increased sales, accelerated demand generation, broader levels of customer loyalty, greater efficiency, and cost streamlining.

Operating costs are reduced for your organization as more customers are willing to take on part of the back-office operations, such as updating membership information, by entering data that can now be fed into a connected data hub.

There is even a reduced cost of customer acquisition. Leveraging the single view is an important step toward making advocates out of satisfied customers. Your advocates become your new salespeople.

With an improved ability to execute on business-critical objectives, organizations can take advantage of this improved use of resources to expand existing strategies and replicate execution in new strategies.

Data stored in the single view can be used to enrich back-office processes such as product development where implicit and explicit customer preference data can be leveraged. In addition, the data enables you to identify your most valuable customers as well as customers with the greatest potential. Leading-edge companies demonstrate that superior customer experience leads to competitive leadership and even domination.

An increasing number of companies are tapping into the habits of connected customers. According to one study, 36 percent of U.S. organizations interact with customers and prospects in five or more channels. On average, large companies operate through four channels. The most common channel for interacting with consumers is online through an organization's website, with 72 percent of respondents citing this channel.[5] But just because a company communicates using multiple channels, this does not mean that it is creating cohesive, relevant, connected customer experiences. In fact, the opposite may be happening.

WHAT YOU NEED TO DO

What does it take to build a single view of the customer? The basic idea of a 360-degree view of the customer is not a new notion. But what is new is the rapidly evolving shift to digital that is currently transforming the playing field on which brands attempt to attract and win customers. The ability to create high-quality customer experiences—in real time based on data—is now essential in combination with the single view of the customer.

Before diving into what you need to do, let's clarify a bit further what we mean by the term *single view of the customer*. We define single view of the customer as the ability to create a connected data model that you can use to store hierarchical information (for example, identity, digital behaviors, digital interactions, and meaningful responses) for individual customers. We take the definition a step farther and include an ability to systematically leverage the stored data to facilitate— progressively in real time—relevant online and offline experiences for the purpose of achieving marketing objectives (and other types of business objectives).

Our definition of single view of the customer also includes an ability to leverage the data in real time and for analytical purposes. Figure 10.2 shows a variety of life cycle interactions and touch points that provide data sources for the single view. For example, the data store and infrastructure should permit the ability to capture and track

Social
contributions

Acquisition
sources

Interactions

Campaign
responses

Advocacy

Acquisition

Community
contributions

Completed
goals

Social
shares

Profiled
behaviors

Utilization

Community
transactions

Explicit
preferences

Service
transactions

Usage
transactions

Figure 10.2 How Customer Life Cycle Interactions Enrich Data for Marketing's Single Customer View

an interaction in a social channel and then use that interaction for the same person should that person visit your company website through a social channel. When this happens in one journey, you need to capture and store the social platform interaction and then, as the website visit progresses, use the social interaction to present relevant content and calls to action that continue to nurture the visitor.

What's more, an essential part of our definition of the single view of the customer is the ability to connect data. For example, with the ever-increasing use of online advertising, marketers are presented with opportunities to target and retarget on different advertising platforms. The platform used to manage your single view of the customer should support the ability to connect to advertising platforms so you can target customers across any channel.

Other examples of where marketers may want to connect their single-view data repositories are customer relationship management (CRM) systems, point of sale (POS) systems, membership management systems, or customer transaction data warehouses. The criteria for which specific data to connect comes down to questions such as: What data do you need to create a more relevant experience? What do you need to increase trust? And what do you need to nurture your audience?

With this definition in mind, how can different types of businesses leverage a single view of the customer? What types of data can be collected and connected to provide enriched customer experiences? Here are some.

Type of Business	Examples of How to Leverage a Single View of the Customer
Subscription-based business models	A cellular phone operator uses online advertising and social media word of mouth to attract customers who need a flexible data plan. When prospects respond to these online ads and become customers, the single-view database stores the customer attribution factors such as the psychological need in the ad the person responded to, the channel used, and any social connect data that may have been acquired. When the mobile phone company wants to later up-sell to this customer, the company uses the customer data combined with transactional usage data to identify target customers. The customers are targeted through the cell phone company app on their cell phones.
E-commerce	An e-commerce luxury clothing merchandiser uses its single-view database to combine website visitor behavior with data on recency and frequency of purchases. The combined data is used to dynamically merge relevant content into email marketing messages. These messages are sent based on recency of last website visit or latest purchase.
Retailer (bricks and clicks)	A consumer health care chain designs its single view of the customer in combination with a loyalty card program. Data in the single-view database captures preferences and behavioral profiling from the customer's online activity. This includes extensive lifestyle content. When the customer is making a purchase in one of the company's stores, the customer's loyalty card is swiped at point of sale. The shelves on either side of the POS counter are stocked with goods planted for cross-sell and up-sell. Based on the customer's online behavior, the sales associate is prompted to try to cross-sell an item in the rack next to the POS counter. The customer can decide to buy nearly instantaneously. Printed material, sent via

(Continued)

Type of Business	Examples of How to Leverage a Single View of the Customer
	automated postal mail, can be personalized based on online behavior and the history of transactions.
B2B	A software-as-a-service company designs its single view of the customer so that it can score the overall quality of each customer throughout the full Customer Life Cycle. It does this based on the customer completing a primary objective at each life cycle stage. The data for calculating the overall score includes a digital channel activity score as well as a CRM activity score. The overall score is maintained in the CRM system and is configured to decay as scoring activities fall off. A key component to the scoring mechanism is the ability to compare prospects who have the potential to increase in value against existing customers who have already reached a target value. During the presale stage the overall score shows prospects who are most likely to buy, during the first-year customer stage the scoring shows customers who are most likely to be retained, and for maintenance customers the scoring shows customers who are most likely to advocate.
Hospitality	A supplier of food and nonfood products to hotels, restaurants, and caterers supplements its single-view data with profile data. The profile data is used to identify website and e-commerce visitors who demonstrate behaviors indicating a potential high-end purchase. This data is used in real time for cross-selling as well as for segmenting subsequent outbound messages.
Not for profit	A charity organization that solicits disaster relief donations on its website sets its single view to capture visitor touch points for website visitors who become donors. The touch point data includes channels of attribution (online advertising, QR codes, social platforms, email, mobile, etc.). The charity uses these points of attribution to target existing donors in their channel of preference. In addition, the charity uses behavior targeting (based on website visit profiling) to target cohorts of existing donors in their respective channels.

CREATING A SINGLE VIEW OF YOUR CUSTOMER

So what does it take to develop and leverage a single view of the customer? The first step is to define an overall approach. Depending on the type of business you work in, the approach may consist of defining a vision, strategy, capabilities, metrics, as well as setting priorities.

Your vision should describe the new universe where your company provides customer experiences driven by technology. As with any successful strategy for organizational change, you must be able to create a vision of what your organization will look like when it uses a single view of the customer. Sit back and imagine the ultimate customer journey as it is propelled by customer-centric values such as convenience, service, time savings, cost savings, and access.

Your strategy for establishing the single view of the customer should ideally start with an analysis—internal and external. This analysis should include feedback from existing and potential customers regarding what makes a quality connected customer experience. Remember the value of walking a mile in the customer's shoes. Too often companies create customer-centric processes that benefit the company more than the customers.

The single view of the customer requires shared data across many business units. Different parts of the organization will need to agree on issues large and small—potentially down to details like multicultural salutations and gender types. Where to define the boundaries of what is included and excluded is an important part of the strategy. For a given business, the single view of the customer may be defined as existing and potential customers and the digital channels they touch, and may include all data from inbound and outbound communication and touch points.

When considering capabilities, keep in mind the real-time nature of cross-channel, connected engagement. Capabilities you should consider include core functions such as the standard data fields in the customer record, the maximum number of custom fields, field types, data field masking, and the wide variety of data value types that will be stored and used in, for example, segmentation. Unicode support is another consideration to manage customer profile data used across different geographies. Your approach should take into consideration that you should continuously enrich data by storing key responses and interactions.

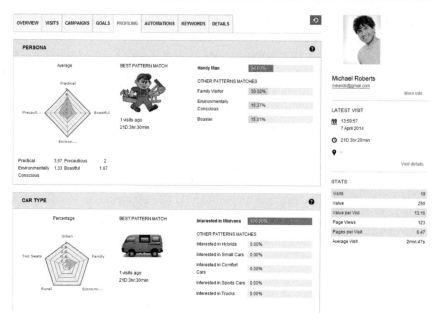

Figure 10.3   Example of a Record for a Single View of the Customer

As shown in Figure 10.3, consider storing data such as website visit details, historical website interactions, attributed campaigns, persona matching, and a variety of data field values.

When defining your single customer view, it is important to consider connecting to other data sources. How to connect and what to connect are important questions. For example, if you want to support campaign segmentation based on the recency and frequency of customer purchases, you may need to connect to a database that stores customer transactions.

A key capability you will need to address is the accessibility of the shared data; accessibility may include requirements like high-scale, high-speed access, geographic reach, and so on. In many cases, cloud-based availability is an ideal solution as long as the cloud system supports on-demand scaling and high-performance responsiveness needed for behavioral targeting in multi-touch customer journeys.

Governance of the single view of the customer is essential. Your approach should address issues such as what is the unique key for matching and updating, management of duplicate records, and consistent campaign attribution schemes. An essential aspect of governance is establishing and enforcing a consistent naming taxonomy (as described in Chapter 8). Each time a marketer creates a campaign, an email, or inbound URLs, for example, the name should adhere to a taxonomy. The structure enables you to more readily analyze and compare results for marketing initiatives.

Another important planning consideration is what metrics you use to measure effectiveness. You want to identify how you will measure the value of individual members of your single-view database. Depending on the type of business you operate, the measurement methodology can vary. In addition to the Customer Lifetime Value metric described in Chapter 2, here are some examples to consider:

- *Engagement Value*. This metric for engagement enables you to understand and compare customer outcomes. As discussed throughout this book, this metric provides insight into campaign attribution, channel attribution, and visitor interactions. When considering the single view of the customer, Engagement Value provides a metric for determining the overall value of your customer base.

- *Activity score*. When you want to score the quality of website visits based on specific interactions as well as explicit data captured, you should have the capability to establish a flexible visitor scoring scale. Ideally, a wide variety of interactions—such as page views, downloads, game plays, and tool interactions—can be combined with a counter mechanism. You can also think of this as a readiness score. Data values in web forms submitted by visitors should also be able to increase the value of a visitor activity score. The mechanism should provide the ability to apply formulas to increase or decay an activity score automatically based on conditions such as the passage of time where no activities occur.

- *Recency, frequency, and monetary scoring*. Depending on the type of business you work in, you may find that it is useful to score customers based on recency, frequency, and perhaps the monetary value of certain transactions. With this type of score in place, you can segment your audience and cross-correlate with channels of attribution and behavioral profiling to understand what factors drive, for example, buyers who make expensive purchases at a given frequency but have not made a purchase recently. Inbound personalization could be used to target this segment, as well as outbound email or smartphone messaging.

Finally, an essential part of defining your approach to attaining the single view of the customer is prioritizing capabilities based on need, cost, and time. Very often, the process of prioritization amounts to weighing trade-offs. Here is a short discussion of some of the universal issues that you may find yourself wrestling with when defining your approach.

- *Ease of execution versus degree of customer relevancy.* Especially in global companies where the marketing tools and skill sets in regional marketing departments may vary, regional offices may have a limited ability to execute using data in the single-view data store. In these situations, companies should strive to avoid the lowest common denominator factor from limiting the customer experience outcomes. Steps to lift the capabilities of local marketers include role-based training, establishing a centralized service center, providing a marketing taxonomy guide, and maintaining updated online documentation describing marketing user processes.

- *Centralized versus decentralized.* For geographically dispersed businesses, defining a single view of the customer involves supporting multiple languages, cultural variances, and local sales and marketing practices. In some cases, it makes sense to develop a core data model for the universal single view of the customer and provide the ability to enhance the core using additional tables or entities of data.

- *Time to market versus quality.* Developing a single view of the customer is typically a complex undertaking. Your original plan should include quick wins. These can help reinforce commitment and increase momentum.

- *Big data versus smart data.* Is it the amount of data or the quality (granularity and age) of data that makes heightened customer experiences? When considering what data to collect and connect, prioritize the data that will most readily contribute to relevant customer experiences in key phases such as awareness, research, and decide. Often this is data that can be used to increase relevancy for calls to action for valuable goals and the content used to reinforce these calls to action.

BREAKING BARRIERS

At the outset, the prospect of creating and leveraging a single view of the customer may seem a colossal task rife with internal and external challenges. However, as leading-edge companies demonstrate, it can be done. For sure, it is not easy. So what are some of the barriers companies may face when developing and utilizing the single view of the customer, and what are some of the ways these barriers can be overcome?

In surveys where marketers are asked to rate barriers they face to improve marketing outcomes, lack of budget and resources is commonly many marketers' number one barrier to success. But when you dig deeper into these surveys and compare the types of businesses that these marketers work for, you see an interesting pattern emerge. Marketers who work for online business tend *not* to cite lack of budget as the top barrier.

Why is this? One key reason is likely the inherent support by executive management for strategic marketing initiatives in online businesses. By their very nature, online businesses understand the commitment, competencies, and mind-set needed to build a digital practice. According to our research as well as other research, online businesses are the most digitally mature. Other types of companies—especially those with traditional business models—should seek to learn from the habits, practices, values, and cultures of successful online businesses.

People Barriers

It takes more than learning from the habits of online businesses. Most companies have to deal with their own baggage—the legacy of being a nondigital business in an increasingly digital world. Herein lie additional barriers when it comes to attaining the single view of the customer. Take customer personas, for example. These are an essential part of using behavioral profiling.

Challenges may arise when stakeholders from different parts of your company come together to identify the primary characteristics and motivational triggers of buyer personas. The key to overcoming such a challenge is first to anticipate the debate and to be prepared to establish a framework that focuses on common persona characteristics. Thereafter, the focus can turn to the variations for different business units.

Technology Barriers

From a technical perspective, barriers you may face include integration challenges, master data management, and scaling your infrastructure. Master data management—technology, tools, and processes required to create and maintain consistent and accurate lists of master data[6]—is an essential practice to retain customers for life. Failing to update a customer's new address in a timely manner can result in not only a lost customer but also negative backlash in social media communities.

When approaching the question of master data, you must have a clear focus on what data provides relevance and what data is needed for integration. When generating relevancy, a powerful source is a customer's most recent behavior balanced against past behaviors.

Scalability can be another barrier. The option to run the database in the cloud is essential. The database should be able to store high volumes of data and provide flexibility in the types of information that can be captured and stored while keeping the ability to deliver local experiences.

Organizational Barriers

The ability to execute using the single view from a sales and marketing perspective is another potential barrier to success. There is just too much to do for most marketing organizations. Marketing has to contribute not only to establishing the single view, but also to executing well-orchestrated campaigns. One negative side effect can be structural silos where different marketing groups in the organization "own" certain touch points with the customer but are not coordinating efforts (or customer data). Marketing's ability to execute using the single view may be hampered by this negative side effect.

Many organizations will need to establish a new, more disciplined culture in the marketing organization in combination with developing new marketing technology skills.

Customers want the companies they deal with to act as one. They want unified, connected experiences that don't derail. No doubt, for most companies, the challenge of establishing the single view of the customer requires core changes. You must plan for how you will help your organization adapt to the new culture needed for a single view of the customer.

Moving to the Higher Level of Engage

Mastering the Engage stage requires a combination of capabilities and disciplines. Let's consider:

- What types of competencies are needed?

- How long will mastery take?

- How will you know when you have achieved the single view of the customer?

For many companies, the act of establishing the single customer view requires transforming their businesses. This transformation may be part of a company-wide effort to become customer-centric. With the emergence of digital channels, businesses are rethinking the role of marketing and how businesses provide customer experiences. One result is the emergence of positions such as chief customer experience officer, as well as heads of customer experience strategy and customer experience intelligence.

The purpose of these roles is to develop an outside-in approach to providing consistent, contextually relevant customer experiences. A key responsibility of the chief customer experience officer is driving organizational change in how customer experience is managed. Companies that have not yet established ownership of the customer experience can still take significant steps. For example, start by aligning functional objectives across two or more functions (sales and marketing, for instance) and appointing owners for cross-functional goals, such as benchmarking and ongoing measurements.

The farther you move up the Customer Experience Maturity Model, the more important specialization becomes. As one senior marketer put it, in the quest for the single customer view, what is essential is the "true marketing technologist." The tools and technologies exist. It's mostly a question of finding marketers with the right skills.[7] For an increasing number of companies, this is evident in the role of the chief marketing technologist.[8]

A key question to include in the discussion of staffing is the integration of marketing teams. One study showed that only one-third of marketing teams are integrated. The same study showed that integrated marketing teams execute twice as many integrated campaigns as nonintegrated teams.[9]

How Long Will It Take?

How long will it take to attain a single view of the customer? Generally speaking, it is a journey that could take some companies months and others years. Although our research shows that a minority of organizations have a single view of the customer, most organizations will eventually attempt to create the single customer view.[10]

Part of the answer to how long it will take depends on your starting point. For example, does your company have a customer experience vision and strategy—designed for the connected customer—that spans the organization? Other key factors that influence how long it will take include:

- Does your organization design cross-channel customer journeys that are customer-centric?

- Have you identified and collected the data that will be most effective in generating consistent cross-channel customer experiences?

- Have you identified and designed internal processes to provide customer-centric experiences?

- Can your current infrastructure of customer touch points collect the necessary data and give you the ability to generate real-time customer experiences?

- Have you designed and deployed processes to analyze and model customer behavior as well as generate customer-centric dialogues?

- Is your single customer view data standardized, accurate, and cleansed?

- Do you have the staffing competencies in place to collect, connect, analyze, and utilize data—that is, historical data as well as real-time data?

How Do You Know You Are There?

How will you know when you have reached the Engage stage? One simple test is the mission statement that your company uses—for example, the statement in your report to stakeholders. Consider Amazon.com's mission statement: "to be Earth's most customer-centric company." If the mission statement for your company is not customer-centric, then you may not be on the road to customer experience nirvana.

A mission statement may just be writing on a piece of paper. The real test of whether you have reached single customer view Valhalla is to look at your business results. Typically, successful customer-centric initiatives lead to results such as:

- New revenue that can be attributed to integrated activities using the single view of the customer

- Increases in campaign response rates and conversion rates

- Increases in the number and value of products used by an individual customer

- Quantified identification of new potential revenue

- Improved decision making from more accurate, centralized data

- Execution of a greater number of marketing campaigns that result in high-quality leads being routed to sales

- Measurable improvements in customer satisfaction

- Increased social messages regarding positive customer experience anecdotes and sentiment

- Reductions in overall customer attrition as well as fewer product and service abandonments

One way to know when you are there is to "walk a mile in your customer's shoes" (remember our "Communicate with Intent" test in Chapter 1) and evaluate your experience. Start an undercover customer journey just as a potential customer would. First search online for recommendations and reviews. Visit your website as a potential customer might—by clicking on an online ad or clicking on a link. Subscribe to your email publications. Click into your website and begin your search as a potential customer with the positive and negative reviews in mind.

You should begin to see signs that your experience is not the same as the experience for all other potential customers. You should begin to see messaging and content that recognize how you came to the website and why. You should feel your level of trust increasing. Behind the scenes, the database platform containing the data for your single customer view should be working hard to give you a better experience.

As your journey continues, using different visits on different devices, you should recognize a two-way dialogue being established. When you are presented with a call to action, it should be relevant. When you respond to a call to action and provide data, you should recognize when the data is used to provide a greater degree of relevancy. Continue your journey using the touch points as if you were a real prospect or customer. Evaluate whether connected data is used effectively to further make your experience more relevant and increase your trust.

Perform the same undercover exercise as if you are in the shoes of a new customer and a longtime customer. Is historical and real-time data used to provide a cohesive brand experience across channels? Is this data stored or connected in your single view of the customer? If yes, congratulations! Your marketing organization has mastered the Engage stage. You are ready to depart the staging ground for the high altitudes of the next level, Stage 7—Lifetime Customers.

NOTES

1. "Multi-Channel Data Deluge Drives Higher Consumer Expectations, Experian Research Reveals," www.experian.co.uk/marketing-information-services/scv-press-release.html.
2. Ibid.
3. Ibid.; Paula Rosenblum and Brian Kilcourse, "Omni-Channel 2013: The Long Road to Adoption: 2013 Benchmark Report," Retail Systems Research (RSR), June 2013, www.slideshare.net/Ikusmer/omnnichanel.
4. "Ensuring an Omnichannel Customer Experience: An Experian QAS White Paper," Experian QAS, 2012, www.ngretailsummitus.com/media/whitepapers/2013/DQ_Impacts_On_OmniChannel.pdf.
5. Ibid.
6. Roger Wolter and Kirk Haselden, "The What, Why, and How of Master Data Management," Microsoft Developer Network, November 2006, http://msdn.microsoft.com/en-us/library/bb190163.aspx#mdm04_topic4.

7. Lucy Fisher, "Single Customer View? It's the Product, Stupid!," *The Guardian*, March 20, 2014, www.theguardian.com/media-network/media-network-blog/2014/mar/20/single-customer-view-product-marketing.

8. Laura McLellan, "How the Presence of a Chief Marketing Technologist Impacts Marketing," Gartner, January 17, 2014, https://www.gartner.com/doc/2652017/presence-chief-marketing-technologist-impacts.

9. "The Experian 2013 Digital Marketing Report," Experian Information Solutions, 2013, www.experian.com/marketing-services/2013-digital-marketer-report.html.

10. "Building a Single Customer View," Infographic, Experian Information Solutions, 2013, www.qas.com/data-quality-infographics/building-a-single-customer-view.htm?tid=3390.

CHAPTER 11

Stage 7—Lifetime Customers

If you do build a great experience, customers tell each other about that. Word of mouth is very powerful.

—Jeff Bezos, CEO, Amazon.com

O rganizations in this stage optimize the connected cross-channel customer experience by using real-time data and predictive analytics to anticipate the needs of customers and create timely relevant one-to-one dialogue (see Figure 11.1).

THE LIFETIME CUSTOMERS STAGE

Any business that wants to endure and profit must strive to reach Stage 7, Lifetime Customers. But it isn't easy. Reaching Stage 7 can be a long and arduous climb. Your organization's culture must be unified in giving the customer a great experience. All divisions and departments use a single view of the customer that crosses online and offline touch points. The customer experience is aligned with organizational objectives. So giving your customer a great experience drives success in your organizational objectives. Everything you have built in the previous six stages is working together.

In Stage 7 most of your customers are not only loyal to your organization, but they also are active advocates for you. At this stage your customers think of themselves as customers for life.

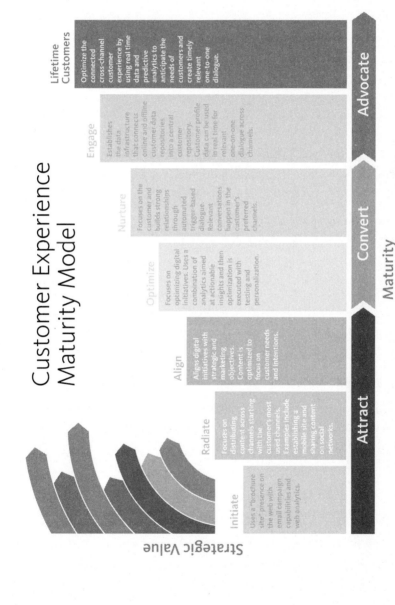

Customer Experience Maturity Model

Strategic Value

Initiate
Uses a "brochure site" presence on the web with email campaign capabilities and web analytics.

Radiate
Focuses on distributing content across channels starting with the customer's most used channels. Examples include establishing a mobile site and sharing content on social networks.

Align
Aligns digital initiatives with strategic and marketing objectives. Content is optimized to focus on customer needs and intentions.

Optimize
Focuses on optimizing digital initiatives. Uses a combination of analytics aimed at actionable insights and then optimization is executed with testing and personalization.

Nurture
Focuses on the customer and builds strong relationships through automated trigger-based dialogue. Relevant conversations happen in the customer's preferred channels.

Engage
Establishes the data infrastructure that connects online and offline customer data repositories into a central customer repository. Customer profile data can be used in real time for relevant one-on-one dialogue across channels.

Lifetime Customers
Optimize the connected cross-channel customer experience by using real time data and predictive analytics to anticipate the needs of customers and create timely relevant one-to-one dialogue.

Attract **Convert** **Advocate**

Maturity

Figure 11.1 Sitecore® Customer Experience Maturity Model™—Lifetime Customers Stage

Author Ron Person relates the following.

In the same week, I had one of the best customer experiences of my life and one of the worst. The experiences were just about as opposite as possible. The week began with the worst experience. I went to a big box electronics store looking for television headphones. After a futile search I saw three salesmen half watching me from 20 feet away. I walked over and asked them for help.

One said, "Headphones should be on aisle 12, bottom shelf. Look there. You'll find them." And they went back talking among themselves. I went back and looked where I had before, but still didn't find them.

Returning to the salesmen, I asked for help again. One of them sullenly walked over, got on his knees, and looked at the bottom shelf. His response was, "Shelf label got knocked off. No headphones, either. Why don't you come back in a week or two?"

No apology, no offer to call me or give me a raincheck. I have told as many people as possible about the service at that store.

Later the same week I drove back from the San Francisco airport and passed Nordstrom. It was about 8:30 at night, almost closing time. I love brightly colored ties and needed a shirt. So I went in. A young man greeted me cheerfully (this in itself surprised me because of the time of night) and asked how he could help me. We talked about his college work and about my consulting as we searched the shirts and ties. No luck! We spent only about 10 minutes together, but listen to what happened later.

Almost a month later I returned again from the San Francisco airport, again late at night. Again I stopped at Nordstrom. Walking down the aisle I was at least 20 feet away from the counter when the same young man looked up and, without checking a smartphone or database, said, "Hi, Mr. Person. I've got just the tie you're looking for." And it was a great tie.

I bought the tie, a shirt, and a pair of slacks. I tell as many people as possible about the service at Nordstrom.

These two stories illustrate the point of creating lifetime customers. Nordstrom is 50 miles from my house. I pass it only when returning from the airport. But, when I need nice clothes, I make a point of checking at Nordstrom. And I spread the word about its great service.

Working through the previous six stages has taken work throughout your organization, but it's worth it. Throughout this chapter you'll read how advanced marketing organizations reach Stage 7 and what it takes to stay there.

Once you reach Stage 7, Lifetime Customers, you've reached the level all marketers aspire to.

Objectives

The main objectives of the Lifetime Customers stage are:

- Create a customer experience so good that customers are retained for life.

- Optimize the customer experiences across all online and offline channels, using real-time predictive automated personalization to offer the most relevant content.

- Maintain competitive advantage by being the fastest and most agile in testing new initiatives.

Amazon.com, an Example of Stage 7 Maturity

Amazon.com is recognized as the world leader in digital excellence and e-commerce. From its proverbial garage start-up in 1994 until now, it has become a $19.74 billion company and clearly defines a Stage 7 organization.

In Amazon's 2008 Securities and Exchange Commission (SEC) filing the company described its vision of the business as: "Relentlessly focus on customer experience by offering our customers low prices, convenience, and a wide selection of merchandise."

Notice that Amazon placed "customer experience" as the keystone of their vision. In order to make that happen they have to have Stage 6 data integration as a foundation and then create customer convenience through their use of predictive analytics. In fact, for 2013 the American Customer Satisfaction Index rated Amazon.com as the leader in customer satisfaction with a rating of 88. The average rating for Internet retailers is 78, with other company ratings such as eBay at 80 and Netflix at 79.[1]

Focusing on continuous innovation and customer experience has not held Amazon back from financial growth. A key metric for online retailers is revenue per unique user, similar to Engagement Value. Estimates by JPMorgan's Imran Khan in 2011 found that Amazon generated $189 per unique user while the next closest competitors were eBay at $39 and Google at $24.[2] That means Amazon generated more than seven times Google's revenue and was magnitudes ahead of other online businesses.

BENEFITS OF LIFETIME CUSTOMERS

The Lifetime Customers stage builds on the foundation and the benefits of the six Customer Experience Maturity Model stages that came before. Reaching this level is an accomplishment that few of your competitors attain. Once here, you have a distinct advantage over competitors. Even more customers become your advocates and market for you.

Benefits to Your Customers

Anyone who shops at Amazon.com or Zappos.com can attest to the benefits consumers get when working with a Stage 7 organization. The organization knows who you are when you contact it. It "knows you" as an individual and has the remarkable ability to predict what you want.

Stage 7 organizations make the customer decision journey frictionless. Customers find it easier to make decisions because predictive algorithms present the customer's best or most probable decision paths in front of them. Customers feel like they are being helped to make decisions rather than being sold.

The organization appears to be a single entity with a single image and brand no matter whether the customer approaches it offline, online, or through multiple channels. Although analysts used to say there is no loyalty on the Internet, that isn't true. Customers of Stage 7 organizations have built a commitment and trust with the organization. The customers of Amazon, Nike, Lego, and Zappos would rather deal with them than a substitute. Customers are advocates for the organization and feel uncomfortable when forced to work with someone else.

Benefits to Your Organization

Major benefits come to organizations that reach Stage 7. Lifetime customers add significantly to the profitability of an organization (or to the achievement of organizational objectives for nonprofits). These benefits come because lifetime customers:

- Repeat purchases

- Require minimal marketing costs

- Do not require recapture

- Advocate for you and bring in new customers

In a longitudinal study, Bain & Company found that, among the most profitable customers, having greater customer loyalty was an important differentiator.

> Small changes in loyalty alone, especially among the most profitable customers, can account for the long-term divergence of initially comparable online companies, with some rising to exceptional returns and others sinking to lasting unprofitability.[3]

Other studies by major consultancies and analysts produced similar findings. Another study by Bain & Company found that a 5 percent increase in customer retention increased profits by 125 percent.[4]

In their book *Leading on the Edge of Chaos* (Prentice Hall Press, 2002), authors Emmett C. Murphy and Mark A. Murphy found that a commitment to customer experience results in up to 25 percent more customer retention and revenue than sales and marketing initiatives produce.

Commitment to lifetime customers creates a more stable business environment. With the connected single view of the customer that comes in Stage 6 and the ability to predict customer sales and support, you can make more accurate predictions about marketing results, customer support costs, budgets, and more. It's easier to see what's coming.

Amazon, in its SEC filings, has alluded to being able to calculate which marketing channels, content, and products produce the greatest impact on business. The company uses that information to make major and minor changes to business. In fact, Amazon does real-time price adjustments on books to get the maximum return. By making minor adjustments on a book's price, it can see the effect on purchase rate. That allows Amazon to adjust pricing constantly to get maximum profit volume.

Many organizations now have product or service calculators online that are doing more than making calculations. Organizations we've consulted with have very cool online calculators that help online customers select:

- A car model, color, suspension, transmission, and trim package

- Insurance options for auto and life insurance

- Payroll changes that calculate tax and cost effects

- Airline and hotel packages that match price, time, and experience

Although these calculators look like they are just helping the online customer make a better decision, which they are doing, they are also capturing data about individual and customer segments. Marketing and product development in each of these examples can examine which selection combinations were tried and which were finally selected. With that type of information in your customer data hub, you have an incredibly rich amount of data with which to design new products tailored for specific customer segments.

Another advantage to having a customer data hub with this rich customer preference data is that your sharp analysts will set alerts to identify changes in trends in customer segments: "We need more ruby-crimson paint for the sedan models," or "We need a low-cost apartment insurance package for newlyweds." In the old world, identifying these new product opportunities or changes in demand took months and sometimes years. At Stage 7 you should be able to identify these changes as they happen and automate insights based on predictive algorithms.

What You Need to Do to Capture Lifetime Customers

For most organizations, the cost of building Stage 7 systems with custom development would be too prohibitive. Few have the in-house technical resources, knowledge, or organizational commitment. The time to leap ahead of the field by building these systems in-house has passed.

Now we need to take advantage of the tools that are built for us. By selecting the right set of marketing and business optimization tools, we can move faster than our competitors. The changes happening in the customer experience management industry with emerging connected platform capabilities are in favor of organizations that jump on board right now.

At this point you have a few critical decisions in your evolution to Stage 7:

- Should my organization decide to market across all channels and develop lifetime customers?

- Which technology vendor should we choose that can take us all the way to Stage 7?

- Are we willing to make the people, process, and organizational changes to create a great customer experience?

- If we decide not to move to Stage 7, then what niche market can we capture and defend? And what Stage 5 or 6 level approach can we use?

Amazon and Google had the opportunity and vision of building their own systems from scratch. The time for that strategy has passed. The opportunity now is finding the right partner with technology, people, and processes that can get you to the Customer Experience Maturity Model stage you want.

How to Approach Marketing for Lifetime Customers

Marketing at Stage 7 should involve all customer touch points. Every touch point should have access to the same single view of the customer so customers can have the same great experience at all touch points.

At Stage 7 your organization's culture should be data driven and learning oriented. Marketing especially should be run using the scientific method:

Ideation > Observation > Hypothesis > Test > Modify > Repeat

Using the word *scientific* here doesn't take away the fun and creativity in marketing. It means that after the creative idea or observation, marketing must create a hypothesis (guess) about what will happen. A small test can then be done to see whether the idea works. If the marketing idea isn't effective, it can be modified and repeated until it works better than existing methods. When you identify your vendors, you need to select systems that let marketers be marketers again. The experience platform should do the testing. Information technology (IT) should not be a barrier to this continuous testing and improvement cycle.

In his 2014 letter to shareholders, Jeff Bezos directly addressed this concept of failing fast, failing often, and failing small:

> Failure comes part and parcel with invention. It's not optional. We understand that and believe in failing early and iterating until we get it right. When this process works, it means our failures are relatively small in size (most experiments can start small), and when we hit on something that is really working for customers, we double-down on it with hopes to turn it into an even bigger success.[5]

Identifying Processes Critical to Engaging Lifetime Customers

Even though Amazon had a considerable head start against its online retail competitors, it never slowed its rate of innovation. It continued using the scientific method of creating ideas, testing them, and then adopting the ideas that tested well.

Amazon's testing was not just on the website or in marketing content. The Amazon 2014 letter to shareholders comments on the company's use of the *kaizen* approach. (Kaizen is the practice of gradual and continuous improvement in manufacturing, management, and processes.) That approach produced 280 software updates in one year.

Some organizations adopt *kaizen* as a way of gradually introducing change and ignoring the need for quantum change. That is counterproductive and will kill bureaucratic companies that look only to incremental improvement and refuse to innovate. Notice that *kaizen* in Amazon did not stop massive innovation. Rather it was used to make gradual improvement in working systems. Quantum and massive change continued, such as with the Kindle, as a way of leapfrogging the competition.

Cross-Channel Marketing Portfolios

Cross-channel marketing is a natural part of Stage 7. Stage 7 organizations should not have silo marketing programs that operate autonomously. Surveys show that 77 percent of marketers agree they can drive more sales and profits using a balanced cross-channel marketing strategy.[6] A balance should be maintained across all channels to achieve the desired impact at the lowest cost. It's like making a fine meal. Adding more wine to a sauce just because it is an expensive wine does not guarantee the meal will be better, but it could waste the wine.

By the time you approach Stage 7 your organization should be balancing cross-channel marketing using Value per Visit as a metric to compare marketing efficiency in channels. The use of Value per Visit from Stage 3, Align, along with Return on Marketing Investment (ROMI), gives you the information you need to manage cross-channel marketing as a single holistic entity. Without Value per Visit and ROMI you can only manage the individual channels as independent silos and cannot see how they compare in marketing impact or efficiency.

As a marketer you should first estimate what percentage of your marketing should go to each channel. Your marketing channel mix, how you allocate resources across channels, will depend on the preferred channel for the audience, the competitor's strategy (do they already dominate a channel?), and your marketing strategy. For example, if you are a B2B selling industrial chemicals, most of your marketing will go to emails describing new information and informative content by thought leaders. However, if you are targeting millennials (those born during the period from the early 1980s to the early 2000s) with a trendy product, you will need to focus on social channels, word of mouth, and trendsetters related to that trend.

At this stage you have more than Value per Visit as a metric to balance resources and efforts between channels. Although Value per Visit measures the efficiency of your marketing, and you can compare it between channels, it doesn't tell you anything about costs or Return on Marketing Investment (ROMI). With the integrated expense and revenue data you are able to calculate with the integrated data available in Stage 6, you can calculate an accurate ROMI for each channel. With that as a guide, you know where to put your next dollar. Value per Visit and ROMI are great metrics for balancing market resources across channels and predicting future revenue.

Mature multi-channel marketers claim to have significantly better tactical results. Forrester Research reports that 40 percent enjoyed a significant increase in marketing-attributed revenues and 69 percent gained more than a 10 percent increase in customer satisfaction scores.[7]

Data-Driven Marketing and Big Data

Stage 7 solutions involve massive amounts of customer contact data at all touch points and stages in the customer's decision journey. Stage 7 solutions can be on premises, but the massive size and speed requirements usually make a cloud-based solution better. On the front end, putting your Stage 7 solution in the cloud reduces requirements planning, IT development cycles, integration problems, and so on. This not only reduces marketing's dependency on IT, but it also enables IT to move out of maintenance mode and work on continuous innovation to advance marketing and improve the customer experience.

There are many advantages to running your customer experience platform in the cloud. Three big advantages are scale, speed, and reduced complexity. First, the data hub you started creating in Stage 6 requires massive amounts of data and integration. Integrating, storing, maintaining, and serving massive amounts of complex data takes a lot of horsepower and scalability. Second, supporting real-time personalization for thousands of customers across multiple channels requires fast data access to massive data sets and extremely fast computational power. And finally, for some vendors and implementations these systems are actually multiple integrated systems, which build out to be very complex.

The huge growth in capturing customer data comes from customer data being captured at almost every customer touch point. Currently B2B and retail are capturing customer data across, among others:

- Web

- Email

- Social media

- In-store (using Wi-Fi or iBeacons)

- Radio-frequency identification (RFID)

- Point of sale (POS)

- Consumer panel data

- Data-sharing cooperatives

Big data and big analytics must go together to give you the ability to find the unknown unknowns. Unknown unknowns are the events and patterns you can't predict or hypothesize. They are the highly profitable customer segments that no one foresaw.

Eric Siegel in his book *Predictive Analytics* (John Wiley & Sons, 2013) tells stories of how big analytics combines with big data for marketers. He describes the now-famous story of how marketers for Target stores began sending ads and coupons for baby items to a 16-year-old girl. Target's big analytics had detected that her purchases indicated she might be pregnant. Her irate father complained to the store manager. The following week the father apologized to the store manager, saying that he had not been aware that his high-school-aged daughter was pregnant. (Target had been aware, however, because of its analytics.)

Another case is that of Tesco, one of Europe's largest store chains. Tesco sends personalized coupons to both online and offline customers based on their predicted needs. One of our European executives was a target of Tesco's analytics when he received a passel of coupons and discounts for all the items he normally purchased. He had been traveling for a few weeks. The store detected his absence and sent him packets of coupons and discounts for the things he purchased most at Tesco. It was casting lures to bring him back into his local store.

Multiple vendors are developing analytics to work with big data. The analytics you select need to meet three requirements:

1. Publish management and executive reports accessible at any time and in any place. These reports access the known knowns (predictables) and the known unknowns (alerts about anomalies). Managers and executives don't need a great deal of drill-down or ad hoc capability, but they do need access from their mobile devices.

2. Create and publish operational marketing reports about known knowns and known unknowns that enable marketers to optimize their marketing. These operational reports and dashboards need to work at two levels. The basic level makes it easy to create predefined dashboards used by marketers and channel managers. A more advanced level allows operational analysts to drill in and discover solutions to operational issues. It is critical that any analytics system be able to group and correlate data so that you can identify your persona used in personalization and test the results of marketing that targets that persona.

3. Allow in-depth data science. At this level, experts in statistics and predictive analytics use big analytics to find unknown unknowns and discover hidden patterns that could be new fields of gold.

Personalize All Touch Points

At Stage 7, Lifetime Customers, the customer is not only expecting a response that is personalized and appropriate to the context, but in many cases she is also expecting a prediction or recommendation that will help them. It's your marketing and prediction engine's ability to remove some of the friction from life that will keep your customers coming back.

Personalization at this point is a big job, with customer touch points ranging from web to mobile to point of sale to social connection from friends to who knows what in the future. Again, the requirement here is to have a single view of the customer that any touch point can access in real time, find the message for the individual's persona and context, and then respond—all within a second. Systems like this are not science fiction.

In Stage 7 the predictive personalization system you select should go beyond just publishing personalized content through a preferred channel. At this stage the system looks at the historical data for a customer, calculates which content and channel will produce optimal results, and then delivers optimized personal content through the optimum channel for the customer.

Optimizing content and channel is accomplished through a combination of examining historical data and iterative comparison testing, much like multivariate testing of items on a landing page. However, this is like multivariate testing on steroids at the macro level. Developing a system like this in-house is difficult. Your solutions vendor must have this on its development road map.

Making recommendations about your customer's next steps or next purchase requires analysis of many patterns and large data sets. You have two choices:

1. If you are not using predictive systems, you can narrow the choices available to your customers and then use A/B testing to determine which choices give the results you want. In smaller or niche businesses where you have less complexity and high customer knowledge, this is an acceptable choice. You can make and test a few hypotheses and serve your customers well. The downside to this solution is that if you expand your products or customer persona, the system complexity increases geometrically.

2. If you are using predictive systems that analyze big data, then the system can automatically analyze and recommend products or solutions. This is necessary for organizations that have many products or services, many customer personas, or many lines of business.

As Amazon.com has demonstrated, to our chagrin and delight, making great recommendations increases the number of purchases and increases customer loyalty. That big wish list we share with Amazon is not only an offload of memory from our brains, but a data dump into Amazon of where our interests lie and what we are most likely to purchase in the future. Amazon's use of predictive analytics has extended this "future service" even farther. In 2014 they filed patents for anticipatory shipping, shipping goods to customers before the customer orders them.

The Power of the Connected View

Another example of the power of having a connected view of the customer comes from Sitecore. Sitecore's marketing strategy is designed to make every touch point with its customers relevant and to go the extra mile. Sitecore has many interactions with customers across many touch points, such as web, mobile, social, email, and third-party sites.

Offline customer touch points that Sitecore wants to track include phone calls, meetings, marketing events, and so forth that are handled by different teams, from sales to customer enablement.

To make sure that the conversation across these different touch points and teams remains relevant, Sitecore architected its system to have a single view of the customer, gathering all possible data available. This single view of the customer is typically established when a contact record is created. That contact or person could have many different previous interactions, all anonymous and across different channels.

By storing all the customer touch point data for different interactions, Sitecore is able to match the contact with their previous interactions. This gives Sitecore a better understanding of customer intent and channel attribution. This benefits the customer by making future contacts more relevant and timely. It benefits Sitecore because it can understand the channel attribution at different stages in the decision journey—for example, which is the best channel for initial awareness and which is the best channel for key conversions. This makes Sitecore marketing more effective and improves the return on marketing spend.

Based on the single view of the customer, Sitecore can send relevant content across appropriate channels. For example, customers could receive relevant content on their next website visit or could receive relevant contact from someone in customer enablement based on their touch point history.

Having a single view of the customer is powerful, a true win-win for Sitecore and its customers. This single view of the customer has become even more powerful as it is coupled with predictive analytics. A recent example is when one Sitecore executive looked at predictive data, called one of the regional offices, and asked the managing director if a customer had called about a specific topic. Surprised, the managing director responded, "How did you know that? They just called me about this." (The managing director hadn't seen an updated view of the data yet.)

Automatic Recommendations to Optimize Marketing and Forecasting

At the more mature levels of Stage 7 you will implement automated recommendations. This provides recommendations marketers can act on. Stage 7 analytics doesn't present primitive metrics like time on page or bounce rate. Instead, it makes actionable recommendations on search engine optimization (SEO), content preferences by different facets, social intent, campaign improvements, and more. Marketers are able to accept or reject recommendations. For example, a marketer would be given the choice to accept or reject an increase in pay-per-click (PPC) budget on an ad campaign that caused a change of 12,000 Engagement Value points.

Most solutions vendors dealing with Stage 7 companies should supply some level of simple marketing recommendations. However, you need to look for a solution supplier that is looking farther ahead. Once you reach Stage 7, your system has the data and the test results to also make predictions about budget and revenue. Using Bayesian statistics, Monte Carlo simulations, and similar applied mathematics, an advanced Stage 7 system will give your managers the ability to model the effect that changes in budget and channel allocations have on forecast revenue.

Developing these systems in-house takes a tremendous effort and specialized knowledge. Make sure that any solutions vendor you work with has an automated data analysis and recommendation system working or on its product road map.

Breaking Barriers

By the time you begin your move into Stage 7, the culture of your organization should be agile, and data-driven marketing is the normal way of doing things. Your entire organization should be oriented around improving the customer experience.

Management should watch for silos that arise because of politics or metrics that suboptimize. For example, you may have a definition for marketing qualified leads (MQLs) that push prospects from marketing to sales. However, if salespeople won't accept them as qualified leads, they may let the prospects go stale or claim that the MQLs aren't acceptable. Another example is when salespeople are pushed for high close volumes, but the high close volume is achieved with low margins, lack of post-sale support, and subsequent loss of long-term customer value.

Once you have reached Stage 7, the biggest barriers to your organization may be complacency caused by the euphoria of "We are the best!" We've seen this in other leading-edge companies. That attitude, while psychologically uplifting, can take away the competitive edge. You need to continue innovating to improve the customer experience and competitive moat. A good way to promote continued innovation is to foster innovation teams as described in Chapter 12.

MAINTAINING LIFETIME CUSTOMERS

Congratulate yourself and your organization. Getting to Stage 7 is a real accomplishment that only a few in each industry have accomplished. However, your competitors are climbing up through the stages, and your customers demand consistency across all touch points and more and better experiences.

People

Your people and organization in Stage 7 are not normal. As consultants, we've worked in many organizations with many different cultures. Within the first 30 minutes in a new organization it's usually easy to feel the culture. In some organizations everyone in the room waits for the opinion of the highest-paid person in the room before making their politically correct statements. In some the culture is by the book, always using standardized processes. In other organizations, meetings blaze with the fire of new ideas and new processes.

The culture and people in Stage 7 organizations are a mixture. They have well-proven processes that they use for standardized and consistent work. But everyone looks for ways to improve. New improvements in work flow and marketing are tested and the winning methods adapted. Stage 7 cultures and people are continually learning and adapting.

One thing that should be obvious at this point is that the culture in Stage 7 focuses on customer experience. All functional departments share the single view of the customer.

One new skill set that Stage 7 organizations will find difficult to fill is data analyst or data scientist. These are not just traditional web or business analysts. These are statisticians, data scientists, and applied mathematicians who can dive into big data and come up with previously unidentified products, services, marketing strategies, and customer segments.

Process

At Stage 7 you must continue to build an organization with a culture that values innovation, testing, and learning. Stage 7 organizations are continually innovating and testing ways to improve the organization, improve the customer experience, and build the competitive moat. Amazon.com is a great example to follow.

Amazon recognizes that it can't rest just because it is far ahead of its competitors. In this time of entrepreneurial fervor it is death to slow down. Amazon has continued its push by building a competitive moat that may be impassable. This moat is filled with customer loyalty and is as wide as Amazon's rapid pace of innovation. Following its famous (or infamous) 1-Click Shopping patent filed in 1999, Amazon continued with its culture of innovation. The following is a short list of the many innovations described in the 2013 letter to shareholders signed by Jeff Bezos.[8]

Notice that many of these innovations combine to create vertical and horizontal barriers to competitors.

Prime	More than 1,000,000 members by December 2013 use Prime to receive free two-day delivery and access to the Kindle Owner's Lending Library and Prime Instant Video.
Prime Instant Video	More than 40,000 videos and TV episodes are instantly available to Prime members.
Fire TV	Amazon video offerings, including non-Amazon content. ASAP technology predicts what you might watch and prebuffers it. The system even understands voice commands when searching for content. (Notice the use of predictive personalization for delivery of media beyond web content.)
Whispersync	Allows users to switch back and forth between Kindle books and Audible audiobooks without losing their place.
Fresh Grocery	Sells fresh grocery items as well as more than 500,000 other retail items. Currently available in Seattle, Los Angeles, and San Francisco.

(Continued)

Amazon Dash	To make Fresh Grocery even more frictionless, Amazon has invented a wand that users can wave across a retail item at home and the item will automatically be added to the Fresh Grocery list. It's like having your own grocery scanner in your pantry.
Anticipatory Shipping	Amazon has filed a patent for a predictive analytics system that predicts what product purchases will be made in an area in the near future. This enables it to ship items to an area, save on delivery costs, and decrease time to arrival. This is another use of predictive analytics that improves the customer experience, decreases costs, and creates a competitive barrier.

Technology

At Stage 7 marketing is for marketers. The best marketing systems vendors aim not only to solve marketers' problems but to build systems that marketers can use without IT's daily intervention. This leaves IT available to create innovative new tools, not spend time assisting marketing with what should be day-to-day operational tasks. (No marketer wants to wait a week or more for IT to tag content or modify a program just to test a campaign, and any good IT person would rather be creative.)

Systems that have been developed to meet marketers' needs arise from web content management. These customer experience platforms already own the content across the different digital channels. By building on the single view of the customer and connecting to other repositories, they enable marketers to create connected experiences across all channels controlled by the customer experience platform. These new customer experience platforms put marketing in the hands of the marketers.

What this means is that costs are coming down as functionality goes up. At this time most vendors are developing on-site and cloud-based solutions. With the massive amounts of data and more advanced analytics, cloud-based solutions should be considered. Cloud computing enables marketers to focus on their marketing expertise and not on defining system requirements and working with IT. Some of the advantages of cloud-based marketing systems are:

- Systems are quickly implemented and rapidly scalable, allowing marketing to test and innovate without incurring high costs.

- Security is managed by dedicated professionals.

- Costs are less expensive because overhead and start-up costs are distributed among customers.

- Costs are flexible, being dependent on need. You can ramp up quickly.

- Data backup is more reliable with continent-wide redundant systems.

In this new environment, marketing can be left to marketers. IT can work on new innovations. According to Amazon's founder and CEO, Jeff Bezos, technology should focus on innovating solutions for marketing and the customer. In the 2010 Amazon Annual Report, Bezos said:

> Look inside a current textbook on software architecture, and you'll find few patterns that we don't apply at Amazon. We use high-performance transactions systems, complex rendering and object caching, workflow and queuing systems, business intelligence and data analytics, machine learning and pattern recognition, neural networks and probabilistic decision making, and a wide variety of other techniques.
>
> And while many of our systems are based on the latest in computer science research, this often hasn't been sufficient: our architects and engineers have had to advance research in directions that no academic had yet taken. Many of the problems we face have no textbook solutions, and so we—happily—invent new approaches.
>
> … All the effort we put into technology might not matter that much if we kept technology off to the side in some sort of R&D department, but we don't take that approach. Technology infuses all of our teams, all of our processes, our decision-making, and our approach to innovation in each of our businesses. It is deeply integrated into everything we do.[9]

What that means is that although marketing systems may be moving to the cloud, the opportunity still lies with IT personnel to stop doing the maintenance and support they have been doing and focus their talents on extending marketing capabilities.

How Long Will It Take?

If you were developing the systems and processes in-house to try to reach Stage 7, it could take you more than a decade. (It did for Amazon.) However, with the technology from top vendors, and the proven processes and best practices that we've outlined in this book, an organization can go from Stages 1 and 2 to Stage 7 inside of two years. All of this depends on commitment, political will of the executives, and how dynamic the culture is.

The length of time to reach Stage 7 is perhaps not as important as beginning the change immediately. As outlined earlier, you should use quick wins like rules-based personalization, A/B testing, and Experience Analytics to quickly grab executive attention and buy-in. Once you have those, you can present your long-range vision and plan. Chapter 13, Selling to the Board, describes how to sell your vision upward.

HOW DO YOU KNOW YOU ARE THERE?

You have arrived at Stage 7 with lifetime customers when you see an inflection point in customer growth. Marketing is easier because your customers are advocating for you and you can make accurate, data-driven decisions.

Customer growth is organic. A lot of growth comes from word of mouth that is not attributable to specific marketing programs. Your own customers are becoming advocates and spreading the word. Customers reach out to friends and associates to spread the word about what a great experience they have had in their relationship with your organization. They consider your organization as the first choice and accept alternatives only in special circumstances.

Not only do you have a single view of the customer, but your customer has a single view of your organization. The same messages come through all marketing channels and all customer touch points. Marketing messages and branding reinforce around a common experience.

Your customers would feel a sense of loss if they had to deal with a different organization. At this point your organization must keep its competitive advantage by maintaining a high speed of innovation, agility, testing, and redevelopment.

Marketing is innovative and data-driven. It rapidly innovates, tests, and retries. Operational marketing uses analytics and testing for continuous improvement. Marketing software automatically makes recommendations on how to improve performance. Big data is used to identify unforeseen patterns, and customers depend on your recommendations for their decisions.

With accurate data, you can accurately predict growth and costs and have a fairly good estimate of Return on Marketing Investment for each channel and campaign. With this data, balancing cross-channel marketing and setting budgets are significantly easier.

Your people look forward to hypothesizing new marketing programs, setting up a testing protocol, and then testing them. No one moves forward on big marketing efforts until there is data to back up the decision. Test small, test fast, improve, and press on becomes a mantra.

At Stage 7, Lifetime Customers, you have reached the level that marketers aspire to.

NOTES

1. "Benchmarks by Company," American Customer Satisfaction Index, 2013, www.theacsi.org/index.php?option=com_content&view=article&id=149 &catid=&Itemid=214&c=Amazon.
2. "Revenue per Unique User for Tech Companies," Silicon Alley Insider Chart of the Day, January 6, 2011, www.businessinsider.com.au/chart-of-the-day-revenue-per-unique-visitor-2011-1.
3. "The Value of Online Customer Loyalty," Bain & Company, April 2000.
4. "Prescriptions for Cutting Cost," Bain & Company, 2011.
5. Jeff Bezos, "Amazon Letter to Shareholders," 2014.
6. "The Multichannel Maturity Mandate," Forrester Research, May 2012.
7. Ibid.
8. Jeff Bezos, "Amazon Letter to Shareholders," 2013.
9. Jeff Bezos, "2010 Amazon Annual Report," 2011.

CHAPTER 12

Growing Your Organization and Roles

You can design and create, and build the most wonderful place in the world. But it takes people to make the dream a reality.

—Walt Disney

TO WIN, YOU NEED THE BEST RESOURCES

Going through the different stages of the Sitecore Customer Experience Maturity Model, you need to have the right resources on board to help you get the greatest value from the technology needed at each stage of maturity.

The map presented in Figure 12.1 shows the seven stages of the Customer Experience Maturity Model with the capabilities overlaid with the different roles needed at each stage. View the figure in detail at www.ConnectTheExperience.com/cxroles.

In the early stages you can do a lot with generalist marketers, but as you evolve you need to have specialists on board. Specialists can help your organization using the technology to create the connected experience you want to develop for a competitive advantage.

ROLES YOU NEED ON YOUR TEAM

Let's take a look at five of the essential roles shown in the Customer Experience Maturity Model illustration (Figure 12.1).

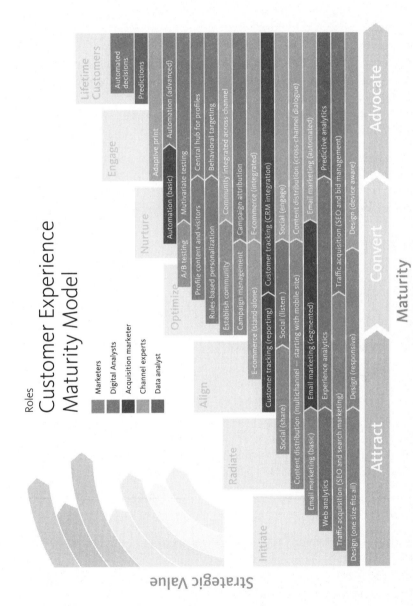

Figure 12.1   Roles Needed for Capabilities at the Different Maturity Stages

Marketers

The role of the marketer is in transition. Marketers must shift to the practice of experience marketing. That means aligning marketing-relevant experiences and content at each stage in the decision journey with how customers decide. As a marketer, the role is more data driven—using data to make decisions on campaigns, influencing decisions on spend, and affecting investments in new initiatives. Being customer-centric, the marketer will look at channels with an eye toward which channels are preferred by the customer and which relevant content is distributed through each channel.

A marketer's key objective is to support the marketing objectives, which are aligned with the strategic objectives. In most cases, one of the objectives is to drive lead generation or contact acquisitions, as this is the first step in connecting the experience across the channels.

Skills and Competencies

- Understands digital marketing and how it contributes to strategic and marketing success

- Experienced with digital strategy

- Strong in communication

- Results driven

- Understands business needs and business models

- Practical

- Marketing presentations focusing on Return on Marketing Investment (ROMI)

Digital Analysts

To be data driven in your marketing, you need to have digital analysts available whose role is to start with a data set and gain insights into the customer's journey, customers' motives, their intent, and how different channels and marketing initiatives perform.

Based on these insights, analysts should present actionable recommendations on how to optimize marketing programs and the customer experience. This task is not just looking at numbers and getting the analytics reports needed for management. Its real purpose is analysis and actionable recommendations. To do this the digital analyst needs to understand the strategic and marketing objectives, the different organizational units that have data available, and how to get that data, as well as to have a keen understanding of the marketing tactics and campaigns.

As a rule of thumb, no matter what stage you are in, if you don't have a digital analyst you should consider this as your top-priority hire for marketing. Unfortunately, the demand for digital analysts is increasing, so they are not easy to find or cheap to employ, but it's worth having a good analyst on board to turn your data into recommendations and actions.

The digital analyst is also the person who can help execute recommendations that include site optimization. These optimization tactics usually include testing and personalization. As your marketing team evolves, so will the roles that split the analyst's duties between analytics and conversion optimization.

Skills and Competencies

- Experienced in digital analytics and optimization
- Marketing technologist skills, including data visualization
- Digital strategy
- Results driven
- Understands business needs
- Practical

Acquisition Marketer

The objective of the acquisition marketer is to nurture leads to become sales ready and support sales throughout the decision journey. Usually, once a contact or lead is acquired the acquisition marketer takes over. However, depending on the size of the marketing team, this role could also be involved in lead generation with a focus on contact acquisition.

The acquisition marketer is expert in designing cross-channel automated nurture flows. The marketer should know the customer's different motivations and intent at different stages and make sure that the flow gives value to the customer.

Primary channels for nurturing are web, mobile, and email—where the triggers could be based on behaviors in any of these channels. The acquisition marketer will also work closely with customer relationship management (CRM) or the customer repository and in the later stages of the maturity model will work with the single view of the customer to look for target segments.

Skills and Competencies

- Experienced with marketing automation
- Experienced with segmentation and data management
- Marketing technologist
- Strongly analytical
- Results-driven
- Understands business needs
- Practical

Channel Experts

Channel experts are expert in their specific channel. Channel experts may overlap across channels, but you will need a unique channel expert for each channel you focus on. Through their expert knowledge of these different channels they are able to influence the channel approach and strategy. They will recommend actions and tactics to get the most out of the channel presence, with the primary focus on the customer experience that drives strategic objectives.

Investing in channel experts makes the difference between doing everything the same as your competitors versus creating a differentiated advantage with tangible outcomes.

Skills and Competencies

- Channel expertise
- Experienced with digital strategy and how the specific channel can be optimized
- Analytical

- Results driven

- Understands business needs

- Practical

Data Analyst or Data Scientist

This role is needed for the higher stages of the maturity model. It is different from the role of the traditional digital analyst. These people are very skilled in statistics and the mathematical algorithms needed for predictive analytics. They are especially experienced working with predictions and identifying customer segments that exhibit similar behaviors where these behaviors can be used to influence the customer's actions. Those in this role should be familiar with the cycles of customer habits, how those cycles can be interrupted and redirected, and psychology buying triggers. Data analysts can use these psychological models when sifting through data to identify key findings.

The data analysts also can help with forecasting and optimizing marketing for strategic impact.

Skills and Competencies

- Advanced analytics

- Predictive algorithms

- Experienced with big data tools

- Forecasting

- Results driven

- Understands business needs

- Practical

EMERGING ROLES

There is a trend for emerging roles that are broader in nature. These are roles that are change agents to help organizations become customer experience–oriented and to align marketing and sales with the Customer Life Cycle.

The Chief Digital Officer or Chief Marketing Technologist

The chief digital officer or the chief marketing technologist is an important role in helping an organization transform into one that is customer-centric. This role has a mandate from the highest executive level to ensure that all cross-organizational projects align with the customer-centric vision and that all parts of the organization develop the single view of the customer.

The person in this role has a deep understanding of how technology can be used as part of marketing, but also how it can drive more value in the organization. The role can be used in some cases to bridge the gap and create collaboration between information technology (IT) and marketing. Sitting at the top of the different organizational units, this role can also launch new initiatives that use technology in new ways and disrupt business as usual.

Experience Architect

The role of experience architect focuses on the connected customer experience as it crosses many channels. This role can emerge from user experience designers, digital analysts, or optimization experts. The experience architect will be the lead in mapping the customer journey with the different stages of the Customer Life Cycle and the different touch points used. This is primarily done through analytics, research, and interviews. Once mapped, this will be used by the experience architect to map the experience through the different channels, assessing which content is relevant and which triggers and calls to action are needed.

The experience architect can help with the creation of personas. Whereas typical persona work ends with the launch of a new campaign or site, the experience architect will actively use the personas to help create the experiences. The experience architect will put the personas through real-time mapping of behavior and content relevant to that persona. Analysis of the results will be used to tailor better experiences and to influence other projects involving those personas.

ORGANIZATIONAL STRUCTURE

A question we often face is how organizations should build the needed teams. In the near term it's important for teams to be agile, prove they can make an impact, and develop a culture and dynamic that are relevant to their charter.

To build your teams, start by examining your current stage of customer experience maturity. Map that against your desired stage of maturity, and look at which roles are needed. Begin with an effort to get those missing staff members on board. Start building a centralized Digital Center of Excellence, and as you grow you can expand this across markets and brands.

Digital Center of Excellence

The Digital Center of Excellence should be at headquarters level, and through its expert resources, its mission is to advise and challenge how connected experiences are created throughout the entire organization and to work with different markets and brands within the organization.

The Digital Center of Excellence should have digital analysts, channel experts, acquisition marketers, and data analysts. Marketers should be at headquarters level and at the different markets and brands.

Through close collaboration between the Digital Center of Excellence and marketing, new initiatives can become best practices that share successful tactics and campaigns across lines of business, brands, and divisions.

As the value of resources in the Digital Center of Excellence increases and the organization matures, this fountainhead of knowledge needs to be scaled, replicated, and distributed to the different regions, brands, and lines of business. The initial owners of this practical knowledge should be the channel experts (e.g., social, search engine optimization [SEO]), acquisition marketers, digital analysts, and data analysts.

Hub-and-Spoke Organization

The hub-and-spoke model maintains a central organization as the main repository of digital marketing expertise. Using the hub-and-spoke organizational model, you can expand the access to this knowledge out to your separate lines of business with their own unique markets and brands. The hub-and-spoke organization employs local resources to focus on specific markets or brands, but it keeps a close connection with the Digital Center of Excellence for best practices.

Typically, local or regional marketing will develop its own specialized expertise in key areas such as social media or SEO. The Digital Center of Excellence is then used to support core and other tactics and initiatives.

In a global organization, having acquisition marketers on local teams helps with the launch of local nurture flows and programs. These local experts are more able to use relevant local content.

Multinational organizations might still use the hub-and-spoke model as the best organizational structure. However, in large multinational organizations there might be a central organizational hub with spokes that then radiate out to regional hubs and spokes. Each hub-and-spoke organization has a Digital Center of Excellence at its center.

THE INNOVATION TEAM

Winning comes by taking advantage of technology to create connected customer experiences driven by deep customer insights. The need for these technological innovations is increasing. The use of technical innovation is a feasible tactic in winning market share from competitors or disrupting business as usual.

To keep innovation going within large organizations, members of the Digital Center of Excellence could take part in innovation projects, making sure that their expertise is used to look into new opportunities in emerging channels or connecting experience in a new way using existing channels.

The more we need to use technology to innovate, the more need there will be for dedicated innovation teams whose core task is launching new initiatives. Even when these projects fail, the innovation teams can bring back the key knowledge and expertise discovered until eventually the project wins and disrupts a new market.

CHAPTER 13

Selling to the Board

There is only one thing more painful than learning from experience and that is not learning from experience.

—Archibald MacLeish

For most organizations, reaching the summit of the Customer Experience Maturity Model requires nothing less than a fundamental transformation. Such change requires genuine commitment at all levels of the organization—from the board to the areas of the business that impact or benefit from connected customer experiences.

In some cases, the need for transformation may originate from the board itself (when we say "board" we mean a committee or group that has been appointed to approve strategic decisions). In other cases, the need to change may originate from within the organization. Either way, the board will eventually need to approve the strategic initiatives and cost. It may be you or a colleague who will lead the charge and make the case. If so, we'd like to give you tools, tactics, and inspiration for selling connected customer experience transformation to your board and management.

REALIZING THERE IS A GAP

The first challenge may be to raise awareness about the gaps in how your company currently provides customer experiences. This includes the customer's experience from first contact through sales and on through the customer's lifetime. The rate at which customers' habits are changing is head-spinning. For many companies, there may be a sheer lack of awareness about the rise of digital marketing in recent years and the resulting consequences to the organization. For other companies, the effects may be more evident in terms of lost sales, sinking market share, and sagging customer loyalty.

Inspiration Workshop

One way to raise awareness about the importance of customer experience is to facilitate an "inspiration workshop" where executives and board members participate. You can use this workshop as a platform to tell the story about the new era of the connected digital customer, their expectations, and how they digitally experience your organization. The workshop can be divided into three parts, with each part addressing one of the following primary questions:

1. How do customers experience our organization today in the different stages of their journey?

2. What are some examples of how we could improve customer experiences?

3. What are some top-line recommendations to moving forward?

To learn more about the inspiration workshop process, go to the book's companion website, www.ConnectTheExperience.com/InspirationWorkshop.

Customer Journey of Today

Begin an inspiration workshop for your management by addressing the question of how customers experience your organization in different stages of their journey. To do that, start by setting the scene from the connected customer's perspective. Illustrate the new habits and practices of the connected customer; refer to industry research as well as data from your current analytics.

In your workshop, show how there is a dramatic shift among consumers to using smartphones and tablets to read email, browse websites, and make online purchases. Show how the rapid adoption rates and growth of social platforms—for example, Instagram, Reddit,

Pinterest, LinkedIn, and Yammer—are important, even for business-to-business (B2B) organizations. Make your presentation personal to the audience by showing how your brand and product/service offerings appear in search engines, online communities, and social platforms. As you do this, keep in mind the idea of walking in the customers' shoes. Get your audience in the workshop to think about what your customers want to experience, what they are looking for, what they want to do, and what problem they want to solve. Find real examples where customers describe intents, needs, requests, questions, comments, complaints, and compliments regarding your brand. Point out to the workshop attendees how these search findings and feedback can be used in your marketing.

Describe how customers embark on decision journeys with the intent of making decisions with the aid of digital touch points. Explain the contribution that positive customer experiences make toward Customer Lifetime Value. Back this up with research that quantifies the value of customer advocacy. For example, reference research that shows how advocates for a company are 5.2 times more likely to purchase again from the company and are 5.8 times more likely to forgive a company when it makes a mistake. Furthermore, use research that shows how customer experience leaders have more loyal customers. Customers are 9.5 percent more willing to purchase from companies that provide superior customer experiences.[1]

Most important, gather data from your current analytics to explain key trends that impact your most important customer segments. This helps executives visualize the impact on real people who represent your customers.

Create a presentation that illustrates to your workshop audience how your customers may not be receiving a memorable experience. For example, you may want to educate them about an important customer segment and then show how people in that segment experience your company's marketing.

Structure your data and presentation to support the story of how customers currently experience your company's digital presence. Create personas for primary segments. Each persona should describe a few main characteristics that represent the segment. Be sure these characteristics include a primary behavior trait and need for relevant products and services.

Use your company's analytics to present the experience from each persona's perspective, not from your company's perspective. For example:

- Customers prefer which channels?

- Customers prefer which devices?

- Customers are attracted by which content?

- Customers are attracted by which online ads?

- Customers who make short visits tend to engage with which content and actions?

- Customers who make average and longer visits tend to engage with which content and actions?

- Customers are more likely and less likely to perform which interactions?

Using selected customer segments, create customer journeys that start with a trigger—a need, intent, or interest. Think of these journeys as the "journeys of today." Mock up the journeys using screen shots. Keep the mockups basic and keep the focus on the overall story. When presenting these journeys, show and describe how a journey may originate in a channel, as well as what the customers experience in each moment and what their intent and behavior in the moment are. As the journey progresses on the website, the visitor may continue to view pages and perform interactions. Focus on visitor journeys that originate with digital ads according to your acquisition strategy. A journey may evolve into a second visit and so on. Visits may be direct or via channels such as email as well.

When the customer journey has progressed, stop and ask questions that lead the board to see the lack of relevance and context for each visitor segment's customer experience. Ask questions such as:

- Does the website treat each visitor the same regardless of the visitor's intent? Point out how the visitor's intent might be revealed at the outset of the visit.

- Are content and calls to action aligned with the buying stages for individual visitors? Many organizations are too focused on stages close to the buying decision, with very detailed product information in those later stages. The majority of visitors, however, are in the very early stages. So there is a gap in meeting and connecting with them emotionally and not just from a product point of view. Point out that this gap represents a significant opportunity.

- Does the website tailor the experience based on any type of segmentation? For example, does it provide the same or tailored experiences for visitors who arrive from specific channels, devices, social platforms, or referring sites?

- Does the website demonstrate that we know the customer? For example, does it recognize returning visitors or email visitors?

- Does the website recognize any preferences that the visitor may indirectly indicate? For example, can we recognize that an anonymous visitor has performed a meaningful interaction on a previous visit?

- Does the website increase the relevancy of the content and calls to action presented to visitors as the customer journey progresses?

- Does the website provide paths for customers who demonstrate satisfaction or dissatisfaction?

When guiding workshop participants through the "journeys of today," present the journeys in a straightforward and unbiased manner. Three or four journeys, each using different customer segments, will probably be enough. Remember, for now you want to show a broad perspective and avoid side discussion that may take you off track. You simply want to show how effectively or ineffectively your company currently provides customer experiences. Executives and boards have an intense, almost painful, focus on bottom-line numbers. If you can show how these changes affect business objectives and the bottom line, you will grab their attention.

Customer Journey of Tomorrow

To address the second question for the workshop (what are some examples of how we could improve customer experiences?), create examples of "journeys of tomorrow." The basic idea is to start with the same journeys that you presented earlier, but this time apply capabilities of more advanced stages in the Customer Experience Maturity Model.

Before presenting journeys of tomorrow, you want to pose questions such as:

- What is the core purpose of our website?
- How do we measure the effectiveness of our website?
- How do we measure the effectiveness of our investments?
- Do different marketing teams share the same metrics?
- How do we measure the effectiveness of the different marketing campaigns, teams, or individuals who work in different digital channels?

Ask rhetorically, "What can we do to increase desired outcomes?" Once you ask this, you can explain the role of contextualization and how increasing relevancy is an effective capability to drive desired outcomes. The flaw with mass marketing has always been that mass marketing communication lacks meaningfulness to its individual recipients.

At this point you may want to very quickly and briefly show workshop attendees the flow a customer should go through from Attraction to Commitment. This flow is described in Chapter 7's discussion of Stage 3—Align, as well as in Chapter 1. This flow is how customers move to commitment and advocacy:

Attract > Communicate > Trust > Commit > Advocate

When your audience members understand this, they can be better judges of what needs to happen at each stage in the buyer's decision journey.

An example of a new journey to show could be one that starts with a need. A customer first performs a search on Google for a product. The displayed results include online ads. The visitor clicks through an ad to the home page of your website (or a landing page). Specific content on the home page is personalized so that it is relevant for visitors who clicked on the online ad or who used specific keywords in the search. (Although this same thing can be done with a dedicated landing page for the search ad, our customers have found through A/B testing that a personalized home page produces better conversions than a product-specific landing page.)

A demonstration sequence might follow these eight steps:

1. Visitor enters keywords in a search engine.

2. Search engine returns results and a pay-per-click (PPC) ad from your company containing relevant keywords.

3. The visitor clicks on the PPC ad and is taken to your home page, which shows a banner ad personalized to the keywords in the PPC and relevant to the visitor's location. For example, a store location might be shown. (Locations are identified using GeoIP services.)

4. As the visitor browses through the website, sidebar elements show high-impact spots relevant to the original search keywords. These could be offers for downloads, videos, webinars, special purchase offers, and so on.

5. The visitor realizes that your website is very relevant and registers to get a download. The system remembers this registration email.

6. The visitor leaves the website.

7. The next time the visitor returns and logs in with their email, the website personalizes its content relevant to the user's prior interests. With more advanced personalization, the visitor will always see personalization and contextualization relevant to the user's most current needs and profile.

8. Marketing automation sends the visitor emails that inform and nurture the user to bring them back for repeat visits.

For the different persona journeys, show how data can be combined with automation to create relevant communication. You could create a combination of mobile visits, email nurtures, and social platform visits that all generate increasingly relevant visits. Show how A/B and multivariate testing can be used to increase outcomes.

At appropriate junctures in the customer journeys, stop and make points such as:

- If potential customers are presented with content that is aligned with their intentions, the customers will likely become more trusting.

- If we show content that is relevant, then potential customers are more likely to stay on our site.

- If customers are presented with calls to action that are in line with their needs and timing, then we are more likely to gain commitment.

- If customers experience that we have an understanding of their interests, timing, and psychological triggers, then it is more likely that we can sell and do repeat business.

- In addition, if customers see that we somehow recognize them—as opposed to treating them generically—then we increase the likelihood that they will return. If we can combine this with other positive experiences, then we increase the likelihood that they will recommend our company to others.

- An important point to make regarding journeys of tomorrow is how to measure effectiveness. Ideally you want to be able to measure it in relation to your key business objectives:

  - The effectiveness of relevancy
  - The effectiveness of personalization
  - The effectiveness of channels and campaigns
  - The effectiveness of content (pages, calls to action, online tools, etc.) with regard to different customer segments

You don't need to go into the details at this point of how such insights are gained; for now, you want to raise awareness about the need for the critical few metrics. You want to make the point that the right metrics are cross-channel and can equally serve the different stakeholders in terms of channel managers and line of business owners. (More about measuring effectiveness will be covered in the next subsection about top-line recommendations.)

Highlight what an improvement there is for customers by using a before-and-after approach. Compare the journeys of today with the journeys of tomorrow, and point out how much better the journeys of tomorrow are for the customer's experience. You should pinpoint areas where the customer experience becomes more engaging and meaningful for the customer and more effective at driving business objectives.

Top-Line Recommendations for Next Steps

Consider using the inspiration workshop just described to raise awareness about problems and challenges related to disconnected and less-than-satisfactory customer experiences. We recommend using these inspiration workshops as platforms for establishing the business case—starting with a clear understanding of the problem. Illustrate the problem and lay the groundwork for the solution, but avoid going into solution mode in this session.

Accordingly, you may want to prepare a list of top-line recommendations for next steps. Based on the discussions and perhaps decisions made in the inspiration workshop, the recommendations may change. In any case, consider using the following top-line recommendations as next steps at the end of the inspiration workshop.

Conduct a Customer Experience Maturity Assessment to identify your organization's current stage. Prioritize initiatives, focus area, and capabilities needed for a phased approach to reach new levels of customer experience maturity. The free Customer Experience Maturity Assessment for this book is available at the book's companion website at www.ConnectTheExperience.com/cxassessment.

Use the approach described in Chapter 7 to explain how to align business objectives and digital goals. Once the objectives and digital goals map are completed, you can focus on specific areas and capabilities your organization needs.

Conduct a Quick Wins initiative where you can create and deploy a minimal implementation of an optimized customer journey. Learn more about how to conduct a Quick Wins exercise at www.Connect TheExperience.com/QuickWins.

You can measure the effectiveness of the optimization as a way of getting firsthand insights into customer experience improvements.

UNDERCOVER APPROACH

If you are in a situation where you do not have the support of the board to make a case for customer-experience transformation, you may want to consider going undercover. With this approach, you demonstrate with small cases how your organization can use the Customer Experience Maturity Model to produce positive outcomes.

The aim of the undercover approach is to secure quick wins. To do that, identify a few calls to action with measurable goals on your website and go through the optimizing process. Within the context of these few goals, you should use the best practices in this book to optimize those goals. Keep it simple and measurable.

Take inspiration from Chapter 8, the Optimize stage. It will show you simple but effective ways you can optimize experiences using personalization and testing. Make sure you record benchmark statistics before and after the optimization. Use the quantified results to help make your case for the board.

For undercover tips and approach, get the latest checklist and inspiration at www.ConnectTheExperience.com/undercover.

THE JOURNEY TOWARD CONNECTED CUSTOMER EXPERIENCES

Naturally, depending on the nature of your company, you will likely identify additional topics to include in the process of selling to the board. But with the approach outlined in this chapter, our aim is to help you take an approach that is outside in. With this, you should be on your way to building a long-term business case and starting your company's journey toward unified and connected customer experiences that are fruitful for both your customers and your organization.

NOTE

1. "Infographic: The State of Customer Experience (CX)," *Direct Marketing News*, October 1, 2013, www.dmnews.com/infographic-the-state-of-customer-experience-cx/article/313996/.

Appendix

About Sitecore

Sitecore is the global leader in customer experience management, delivering highly relevant content, and personalized digital experiences that delight audiences, build loyalty, and drive revenue. The Sitecore® Experience Platform™ delivers one connected experience across both online and offline channels, enabling marketers to own the experience of everyone who engages with their brand and to easily engage in seamless conversations with their audiences when and where they want. More than 3,500 of the world's leading brands—including American Express, Carnival Cruise Lines, easyJet, Heineken, and the L'Oréal Group—trust Sitecore to help them deliver the meaningful interactions that win customers for life.

About Sitecore Business Optimization Services

The Sitecore Business Optimization Services (SBOS) team helps customers and digital agencies achieve business success using the Sitecore Experience Platform. SBOS transfers to our customers methodology, frameworks, best practices, and approaches for people, process, and technology learned with our global customers and digital agencies.

The SBOS team is glad to share some of our best practices and processes with you through this book.

The SBOS Manifesto

We are marketing technologists at heart.

We blend marketing and technology to increase the business value from digital channels.

We believe you can't do marketing if you aren't data driven.

Our first mission is to align digital goals with key business objectives so we can monitor performance and take actions that drive performance improvement.

We start with the question of how to improve business performance.

We search for the relationships between digital marketing goals and organizational objectives; then we use the drivers we find to improve business results.

We are always looking for ways to improve.

Optimization is a continuous process that must evolve with new marketing channels and technology.

We work with committed organizations.

We strive to help organizations break through to higher levels of performance and achieve their goals. We want to work with people who have the same focus and energy we have.

ABOUT THE AUTHORS

LARS BIRKHOLM PETERSEN @LarsBirkholm

Lars Birkholm Petersen is a passionate and innovative senior strategist committed to helping organizations adapt to customer needs by providing strategy and guidance for creating connected customer experiences using innovative technology.

Lars has many years' experience with strategy, marketing, digital analytics, and optimization. He has consulted with hundreds of organizations to improve their use of technology in connecting with their customers.

Today Lars manages the Sitecore Business Optimization Services (SBOS) global team of consultants. SBOS helps customers own the experience across the different channels their customers use. As part of this work, Lars creates processes that support organizations on the road to building lifetime customers.

RON PERSON @SitecoreRon

Ron Person enjoys his work so much he even spends weekends thinking how to create new performance improvement processes. He gets great satisfaction from seeing the people he works with adopt processes that energize and build a better business.

Prior to Ron's position as a senior business consultant for SBOS, he was one of Microsoft's first 12 independent consultants and later used his skills as a Six Sigma Black Belt and Balanced Scorecard consultant to improve organizations in a wide range of industries.

Ron has written 26 books, including four international best sellers on performance improvement and business computing. His previous book *Balanced Scorecards and Operational Dashboards with Microsoft Excel* (John Wiley & Sons, 2013) has a five-star rating on Amazon.

CHRISTOPHER NASH @chrisnash

Christopher (Chris) Nash is a curiosity-driven analog and digital marketer who frequently hangs out at the corner of business and technology. Over the course of his business career, he has advised numerous brands on digital marketing adoption challenges, cofounded a marketing automation company, grown a successful independent consulting business, and traversed the international business arena.

In his current role as senior business optimization consultant at Sitecore, Chris advises customers on strategies and tactics for creating connected customer experiences that produce positive business outcomes. Previously, Chris has held marketing management and digital marketing communications roles at several companies in the United States and Europe, ranging from a Fortune 500 company to technology start-ups.

ACKNOWLEDGMENTS

Writing a book is not an activity that you normally call a *team sport*. In this case, however, teamwork at its best is what made this book happen. As a team of three authors who live 10 time zones apart, we've had our share of virtual passes, kicks, catches, and misses as well as more than a few late night conference calls to cross the finish line. The rewards of close teamwork are unique. We are grateful to have had the opportunity to experience these rewards.

There are many we would like to thank for their support in helping us write this book. First, we would like to thank our colleagues at Sitecore. Many have helped directly and indirectly with answering questions, whiteboarding technical explanations, and tracking down sources. Your contributions have been invaluable. We would especially like to acknowledge those colleagues at Sitecore who played a direct role in supporting this project, as well as those who provided feedback for the manuscript. Thanks to Darren Guarnaccia, Mark Floisand, Mandhir Hazuria, Greg Baxter, Rick Byrne, Sarah McCabe, Beth Torrie, David Williams, Kim Elsass, and Michael Seifert.

We would also like to thank the Sitecore community. This includes customers, digital agencies, analysts, and fellow data-driven marketing geeks. One of the most interesting aspects of writing this book has been hearing the stories of how organizations and agencies use technology to achieve their objectives. The innovative ideas, different points of view, and creative solutions have been fascinating to learn about.

Finally, we would like to thank our respective families. Squeezing in the time to write this book has too often meant that time at home has been squeezed as well. Without the patience, leeway, and understanding of our families, we would not have been able to write this book.

SPECIAL ACKNOWLEDGMENT FOR CASE STORIES

The authors would especially like to thank the organizations, digital agencies, and individuals who helped us with some of the case stories used in this book. These include:

Chester Zoo

Simon Hacking

Digital agency: Code Computerlove (www.codecomputerlove.com)

From Sitecore: Simon Etherington, Steve Renshaw, Phil Scott, and Sandra White

FK Distribution

Tom Jensen

Digital agency: Pentia (www.pentia.net)

From Sitecore: Thomas G. Andersen and Christian Pelle

QT Mutual Bank

Sean Riley

Digital agency: Digicon (acquired by Deloitte) (www.deloittedigital .com/au)

From Sitecore: Rob Holliday and Greg Baxter

Nissan Australia

Heath Walker

Digital agency: Reactive (www.reactive.com.au)

From Sitecore: Rob Holliday and Greg Baxter

Monarch Airlines

Ian Chambers

Digital agency: Codehouse (www.codehousegroup.com)

From Sitecore: Simon Etherington, Steve Renshaw, Phil Scott, and Sandra White

Auckland Airport

Angerie van Wyk

Digital agency: Bullseye Digital (www.bullseye-digital.com)

From Sitecore: Rob Holliday and Greg Baxter

LEO Pharma

Peter Aksel Villadsen

Digital agency: Vertic (www.vertic.com)

From Sitecore: Thomas G. Andersen and Christian Pelle

AustralianSuper

Kirrily Romero

Digital agency: Deloitte Digital (www.deloittedigital.com/au)

From Sitecore: Rob Holliday and Greg Baxter

Connect Websites

Barriers
    www.ConnectTheExperience.com/barriers
Brainstorm method
    www.ConnectTheExperience.com/checklists
Communicate with intent test
    www.ConnectTheExperience.com/CWIT
Content strategy map
    www.ConnectTheExperience.com/SCSM
Customer experience assessment
    www.ConnectTheExperience.com/cxassessment
Customer experience benchmark results
    www.ConnectTheExperience.com/cxbenchmark
Digital Relevancy Map templates
    www.ConnectTheExperience.com/templates
Engagement Value Scale examples
    www.ConnectTheExperience.com/EVS
EVS creation
    www.ConnectTheExperience.com/checklists
Generating digital goals
    www.ConnectTheExperience.com/checklists
Inspiration workshop examples
    www.ConnectTheExperience.com/InspirationWorkshop
Marketing Optimization Matrix
    www.ConnectTheExperience.com/mom
Quick Wins
    www.ConnectTheExperience.com/QuickWins
Roles needed for capabilities
    www.ConnectTheExperience.com/cxroles
Royalty donation to charity
    www.ConnectTheExperience.com/charity
Strategic themes and objectives
    www.ConnectTheExperience.com/strategicthemes
Undercover tips
    www.ConnectTheExperience.com/undercover

INDEX